Free State or Republic?

Free State or Republic?

Pen Pictures of the Historic Treaty
Session of Dáil Éireann

✳

PADRAIG DE BURCA AND JOHN F. BOYLE

*with a series introduction by Fearghal McGarry
and an introduction by Patrick Murray*

UNIVERSITY COLLEGE DUBLIN PRESS
Preas Choláiste Ollscoile Bhaile Átha Cliath

First published in 1922 by Talbot Press, Dublin
First published in 2002 by
University College Dublin Press
Centenary Classics Edition 2015
© Marcus Bourke and the Estate of John F. Boyle 2015
Series Introduction © Fearghal McGarry 2015
Introduction © Patrick Murray 2015

ISBN 978-1-906359-96-6
ISSN 2009–8073

University College Dublin Press
UCD Humanities Institute, Room H103
Belfield, Dublin 4
www.ucdpress.ie

CIP data available from the British Library

Typeset in Scotland in Ehrhardt by Ryan Shiels
Text design by Lyn Davies, Frome, Somerset, England
Printed in Dublin on acid-free paper
by SPRINT-print

CONTENTS

CENTENARY CLASSICS SERIES INTRODUCTION

Fearghal McGarry

'The true history of a passionate period,' wrote P. S. O'Hegarty in *The Victory of Sinn Féin* in 1924, 'cannot be written by any contemporary. We are all too near it.' How does the revolutionary period appear from our present perspective, one hundred years after the Easter Rising? And, now that we have an abundance of 'the necessary documents and data' that O'Hegarty thought essential to write a balanced history, what do the voices of those who lived through this era have to tell us?

Although inevitably shaped by the period in which it was written, the historiography that has emerged over the past century has gradually transformed our understanding of the Irish revolution. The earliest accounts were mostly written by republicans. Popular memoirs by IRA leaders such as Dan Breen and Tom Barry, or the *Fighting Stories* recorded by Irish Volunteers throughout the country, often presented the conflict as a straightforward struggle between the Irish people and the malign forces of British imperialism. The Civil War was frequently overlooked, as were the perspectives of those who did not experience the preceding 'Four Glorious Years' as a period of liberation. This republican narrative was reinforced by school textbooks, as well as by State commemoration which centred on the sacrificial gesture of Easter 1916 rather than the more divisive violence that followed.

From the 1970s, when professional historians belatedly turned their attention to the period, more sophisticated and critical interpretations emerged. Local histories presented a more complex picture of the forces that shaped the conflict. Revisionist accounts emphasised social and political divisions rather than unity, and explored how factors other than patriotism, such as generational conflict, collective pressures and rising social frustrations, motivated many. Against the backdrop of the Northern Irish Troubles, the acrimonious debates that followed revealed a gulf between popular assumptions and scholarly perspectives.

Despite recent controversies centred on revolutionary violence in Cork, this gap has narrowed considerably, as is demonstrated by the transformation of attitudes to Irish soldiers in the Great War. The emergence of a more nuanced understanding of the past is also evidenced by the changing nature of State commemoration (even if this also reflects new imperatives resulting from the Good Friday Agreement, including a problematic tendency to understate past enmities). Notwithstanding criticism of aspects of the government's commemorative programme, the adoption of a 'decade of centenaries' incorporating the campaign for Home Rule, and Irish experiences of the Great War, alongside the War of Independence has enabled a more pluralistic approach than previous major commemorations. So too has the greater attention focused on the role of labour, women and campaigns for social reform.

Another positive development is the widening of access to contemporary sources through such projects as the digitisation of the Military Service Pensions Collection and the 1901–11 Census. Complementing these initiatives, UCD Press's new 'Centenary Classics' series makes available eye-witness accounts of key revolutionary episodes including the Ulster crisis; the aftermath of 1916;

the rise of Sinn Féin; the War of Independence; the Treaty split; and the Civil War. These provide first-hand perspectives on such topics as the significance of sectarian divisions; the impact of imprisonment on republicanism; the importance of popular mobilisation and guerrilla warfare; and the conflict's divisive legacy.

Although most historical controversies stemming from the revolutionary era focus on republican agency, Joseph Johnston's *Civil War in Ulster* reminds us how Ireland was plunged into crisis during a period when republicans exercised little influence. His account of the Home Rule crisis illustrates the role played by Ulster unionists, supported by powerful allies in Britain, in destabilising Ireland before the First World War. Ulster unionist defiance of Westminster, the formation of the Ulster Volunteer Force, and the establishment of a provisional government in Belfast exposed the limitations of the Liberals' Irish policy, not least its self-interested failure to reconcile the democratic demand of Irish nationalists for self-government with the right of Ulster's unionists to determine their own future. The divided loyalties of the British army in Ireland, exemplified by the Curragh mutiny of March 1914; the double standards of the police, seen in the contrasting responses to gun-running in Larne and Howth; and the undermining of the British Government by a Tory party whose incendiary rhetoric and support for armed resistance in Ulster verged on treason, contributed to the failure to achieve a peaceful settlement of the Irish question. Although sometimes interpreted as an irrational response to the Easter Rising, the collapse of popular support for Home Rule can only be understood within the wider context of the Ulster crisis, and the subsequent impact of the Great War.

Like that of other contemporaries (such as the Irish republicans enthused by the Orangemen's success in arming themselves), the perspective of Joseph Johnston – a liberal Ulster Protestant who believed his people could be won round to Home Rule – now seems naïve. However, his repudiation of the Ulster Unionist claim that civil war in Ulster was preferable to the modest reforms represented by Home Rule seems less so, particularly in the context of the 'Home Rule all round' that many expected (and which has since come to pass). In present-day Northern Ireland, where communal identities remain no less entrenched a century later, contemporary resonances can be discerned: the difficulties of sustaining support for political compromise; the pull of sectarian forces towards instability; and the appeal of intransigence, despite its counter-productive consequences, still appear relevant lessons from history.

These accounts offer many insights into the influences that shaped the revolutionary generation. The significance of the cultural nationalist revival is repeatedly encountered. The importance attached to history is particularly striking. The influence of books such as John Mitchel's *Jail Journal* and *Speeches from the Dock*; stories of 1798 and 1867; and memories of the Famine and Land War, is evident, as is the importance of commemoration, most notably of the 1798 centenary which contributed to a wider political revival leading to the formation of Sinn Féin. For republicans like Mossie Harnett and Seán Connolly, the emotional power of the story of Ireland was reinforced by its links with family and local tradition. Much of the success of the Easter rebels resulted from their appropriation of this insurrectionary tradition, and their ability to present it as a viable strategy rather than a vestige of the romantic past.

Marketed as a modern-day *Jail Journal*, Darrell Figgis's memoir of imprisonment also illustrates the republican claim to continuity. As was the case with mid-nineteenth-century Fenianism, propaganda and self-sacrifice were at least as important as revolutionary deeds in cultivating popular support. The first evidence of the republican movement's growing popularity was the success of the campaigns, largely run by women, in support of the 1916 prisoners. The executions of the Rising's leaders, and the subsequent death of imprisoned martyrs such as Thomas Ashe and Terence MacSwiney, reinforced the idea of Britain as draconian and vindictive, and of the insurrectionary tradition as a timeless struggle against tyranny.

The 'cementing of brotherhood' in Frongoch and British jails shaped the emergence of a coherent republican movement. Imprisonment could, as for Michael Collins, enhance one's political prospects or – as with Figgis and Eoin MacNeill – salvage a career blemished by failure to turn out in 1916. Conflicts within the prisons, and the wider support they generated, demonstrate the importance of non-violent struggle after 1916. However, like other aspects of the popular mobilisation achieved by Sinn Féin – the by-elections of 1917–18, the anti-conscription campaign of April 1918, the General Election of 1918 and the establishment of Dáil Éireann in January 1919 – political activism came to be eclipsed by the armed struggle of 1919–21. Revealingly, in contrast to earlier periods when glorious failure and sacrifice were all that could be celebrated, the heroism of IRA memoirs came to overshadow the tragic appeal of prison literature.

The military dimension of the War of Independence is explored closely by two books in this series. Ernie O'Malley's account of Seán Connolly's IRA activities in the midlands and west, and Mossie Harnett's memoir of his experiences as O/C of the West Limerick Brigade's 2nd Battalion, convey the experiences of regional commanders, dealing candidly with the difficult subject matter of ambushes, executions, and the challenges of sustaining support for a campaign of guerrilla warfare. Harnett's account of his service with the anti-Treaty IRA is particularly valuable given his generation's reticence on the Civil War.

Dying for freedom – as Seán Connolly, along with five of his comrades, did at Selton Hill – also entailed killing for Ireland. The price of violence forms a central theme of P. S. O'Hegarty's *The Victory of Sinn Féin* which spans the years between 1916 and 1923.

Believing that politics rather than force should have determined the course of events after the Rising, O'Hegarty attributed the 'moral collapse' of the Irish people to the rise of the cult of the gunman and the horrors of war. Despite O'Hegarty's bleak Treatyite outlook, Harnett's account, conveying his own disillusionment with politics, illuminates many of the same concerns from a different perspective. In particular, the IRA's belief that the politicians had squandered the victory achieved by the gun contributed to the tragic events that followed the War of Independence.

The Treaty debates form the focus of Padraig de Burca and John F. Boyle's *Free State or Republic?* Based on their press reports for the *Irish Independent*, their account complements the spare (and sometimes tediously detailed) transcripts of the debates which are now available on the website of the Oireachtas. Like other first-hand sources, it conveys a sense of what it felt like to be there at the time, describing the changing mood in the chamber, the demeanour of the deputies, the manner in which they delivered their speeches, and their impact; de Valera's words, 'which electrified the assembly', clearly resonated in the Dáil in a way that they do not on the page, a reminder of a charisma of sorts lost to time. The debates divided those who advocated the Treaty as a stepping stone to full independence from those who rejected, largely on moral or ideological grounds, the right of the Dáil to disestablish the Republic. Although some may have trusted Collins's assurances on the Boundary Commission, it is striking how rarely partition features. For Irish republicans, as for British politicians like Churchill, symbolic issues centring on sovereignty such as the oath of fealty, the status of the monarch, and membership of the British Empire, were paramount.

The historian Joe Lee has described the Treaty as the occasion rather than cause of the Civil War. The failure to achieve the Republic brought to a head longstanding tensions within a party which encompassed dual monarchists, pragmatic nationalists, and separatists opposed to any link with Britain. It ignited festering tensions between rival personalities, which became further entangled with issues of political principle. Although often framed as a conflict between supporters of the Republic and those who had abandoned it, the divisions that shaped the Civil War were more complex, with de Valera's proposed alternative to the Treaty repudiated by some anti-Treaty IRA leaders. The factors that determined the stance of ordinary IRA men, which included social and class divisions as well as local rivalries, were not restricted to attitudes to the Treaty.

How do these voices from history add to our understanding of the Irish revolution? Like all useful primary sources, they complicate the picture. One of the greatest impediments to understanding the past is our knowledge of what happened next. These accounts remind us how those who lived through this era acted in the expectation of different outcomes. Prior to the outbreak of the First World War, most Irish people – including republicans – anticipated a Home Rule parliament. The conflict that many feared in 1913 was not between separatists and the British authorities but between the Ulster Volunteer Force and the British army, or between Catholic nationalists and Protestant unionists in the North. Few expected a lengthy war when Redmond declared his support for Irish enlistment in the British army in September 1914.

The value of these texts does not lie solely in the factual light they shed on past events. Like all subjective sources, they are in some respects unreliable, reflecting bias, self-importance or other limitations. Most obviously, they reflect the times in which they were written; O'Hegarty's views on women, for example, have not aged well. As a result, they illuminate mentalities, as well as the memory of the revolution, a growing area of research. Mossie Harnett was one of several thousand veterans who felt compelled to record their experiences for posterity, many doing so in the 1940s and 1950s as they themselves began to pass into history. The realisation that patriots like Seán Connolly – ordinary people who achieved remarkable things – were no longer remembered outside their own townland prompted Ernie O'Malley to write his biographical account. He was also motivated by his concern, widely shared by veterans, that their sacrifices were no longer appreciated or even understood: 'Song and story that once stirred men no longer move a younger generation.' Hence, O'Malley's determination to record, not just Connolly's story, but that of hundreds of unknown soldiers in the final decades of his life, in the hope that their stories could be 'made into a patchwork quilt from memory'. This aim alone provides a compelling reason to ensure the wider availability of eye-witness accounts, particularly during a period of commemoration in which politicians and others will claim to speak on their behalf.

Greater familiarity with contemporary sources, such as the recently digitised witness statements of the Bureau of Military History, should complicate as well as inform commemoration. Although the idealism and achievements of the founding generation will rightly be honoured in 2016, the urge to celebrate independence should be tempered by an unsentimental understanding of the process by which it was achieved. P. S. O'Hegarty's belief that the violence of the revolution killed the spirit of the national movement was shared by many after the Civil War. Violence accelerated the pace of political change, resulting in a level of independence that few anticipated before 1914, but it also narrowed the space for an accommodation between Ireland's different traditions. Despite the relative success of the republican campaign, a significant moment in the global history of anti-imperialism, Irish revolutionaries did not achieve their central aims: the restoration of Gaelic, separation from England (for many, the essence of republicanism), and a united Ireland. Nor did they fully comprehend the contradictions between the last and first two of these aims. Independence, moreover, did not always live up to expectations, as the enthusiasm of the revival gave way to a conservative State. The revolution produced losers as well as winners, including minorities on both sides of the border. It is clear from the Military Service Pensions collection that many veterans endured hardship after, as well as during, the conflict. Few, though, regretted their efforts to achieve the republic of their dreams. Despite the political complexities of the period, and the limitations of their achievements, the revolutionary generation's refusal to bend the knee against more powerful forces will continue to inspire.

Fearghal McGarry is Reader in Irish History at the School of History and Anthropology at Queen's University Belfast. His most recent book is *The Abbey Rebels of Easter 1916: A Lost Revolution* (Dublin, 2015).

NOTE ON THE TEXT

The text of this edition of *Free State or Republic?* with the exception of page 1, which has been re-set, has been printed as a facsimile of the first edition of this book, published by the Talbot Press in Dublin and T. Fisher Unwin in London in 1922.

INTRODUCTION
Patrick Murray

I

On 14 December 1921, the members of the Second Dáil Éireann assembled at Earlsfort Terrace in premises made available to them by the authorities of University College Dublin. Their only business was to approve or reject the Articles of Agreement for a Treaty with Great Britain signed in London eight days earlier by the five plenipotentiaries, all members of the Dáil, chosen by de Valera: Arthur Griffith, Michael Collins, George Gavan Duffy, Robert Barton and Eamonn Duggan.

The debate on the Articles of Agreement was divided between public and private sessions. The press and the public were excluded from the private sessions, thus facilitating more frank and free exchanges than were possible during the public ones. In the course of the first of the private sessions, on 15 December, de Valera put forward Document No. 2, his celebrated alternative to the Treaty. Here he proposed a Republican state externally associated with the Empire, with the British monarch as head of the associated states including Ireland. This innovative, far-seeing proposal, unfairly derided at the time, but which later had a significant influence on Commonwealth relations, was withdrawn by de Valera for lack of general support. The proceedings of the private sessions remained unpublished until 1972. The public sessions extended over twelve days, concluding on 10 January 1922. It is these that form the subject of *Free State or Republic?*

The Articles of Agreement, commonly known as the Anglo-Irish Treaty, signed on 6 December, inevitably failed to satisfy the demands of revolutionary Sinn Féin for an Irish Republic. On the other hand, they represented a considerable advance on all previous British proposals for Irish Home Rule. Those members of the Dáil who supported them could point to the major practical benefits they conferred, above all political and economic freedom for the Free State. They could also argue, with some justification, that the terms being offered were the best Ireland could get; their rejection would mean a renewal of the Anglo-Irish war in which Irish forces were likely to sustain a crushing defeat. Opponents of the Treaty were conscious of the disabling qualifications it placed on Irish independence: the retention by Britain of strategically significant Irish ports, the provision of a six-county secession from the new state, and the consolidation of partition, the continuing incorporation of both parts of Ireland with the British Empire, the imposition of a British Governor-General and an oath of loyalty to the Crown. The more radical Dáil deputies, who preferred principle to pragmatism, or as their opponents would have it, to reality, found themselves conscientiously unable to approve a treaty whose terms violated the oath to the declared Irish Republic taken by all members of the Dáil in 1919.

The closeness of the vote on the Treaty, sixty-four voting to approve and fifty- seven to reject, did not reflect nationalist opinion in the country, north or south, which was largely in favour of the settlement. The Catholic bishops, the press and public bodies quickly, and enthusiastically, called on the Dáil to endorse it. During the Christmas recess, deputies found that their war-weary constituents overwhelmingly supported the Treaty, while its benefits, as well as the folly of rejecting it, were enlarged upon in innumerable Christmas sermons.

The resistance of so many deputies to these influences reflects the strength of radical Republican sentiment in the second Dáil. The members of this Dáil had all been returned unopposed in the 1921 General Election. They owed their membership to an

Irish Republican Brotherhood (I.R.B.) conspiracy controlled by Michael Collins and Harry Boland who had ensured that radical candidates were selected for the 1918 General Election, a policy which saw substantially the same people returned to the Second Dáil. On 7 January 1922, in the course of the Treaty debates, Daniel O'Rourke, a T.D. for South Mayo and North Roscommon, shed interesting light on the process which resulted in his membership of the Dáil. He was, he claimed, elected without his knowledge: the first thing he knew about being elected as a member of Dáil Éireann was to see his name in the public press. Had he known his name was to be put forward he would have objected (Dáil Debates p. 315) Champions of the Treaty in particular were frustrated by the presence in the Dáil of so many members who owed their membership less to ability than to their unyielding commitment to a particularly rigid form of doctrinaire republicanism.

P. S. O'Hegarty argued that the Second Dáil lacked people of ability and independent mind, being what he called "a collection of mediocrities in the grip of a machine", leaving all the thinking to de Valera, Griffith and Collins.[1] O'Hegarty's view seems substantially justified by the tone and content of most of the contributions of the Treaty debates. There are, however, some distinguished exceptions, among them Kevin O'Higgins, Sean Mac Entee and even Mary MacSwiney, although her unrestrained eloquence, extending in the case of one speech over a period of two hours and forty minutes, was more than many of her listeners found endurable. One unkind commentator spoke of her "screeching tirade".

Such was the strength of republican militancy in the Second Dáil that Collins, who had originally played so significant a part in fostering it, quickly realised that if the Treaty was to be approved, he and his I.R.B. friends would have to undermine fundamentalist sentiment by inducing some leading militants to vote for its approval. His success in this enterprise became clear towards the end of the final sitting of the private session of the Dáil on 17 December, when some influential military deputies spoke in favour of the Treaty. Among these were men who had been active in the War of Independence: Seán MacEoin, Eoin O'Duffy, Piaras Beaslaí, Gearoid O'Sullivan, Seán Hales and Patrick Brennan. The contributions of these deputies were persuasive, since their fundamental argument, that rejection of the treaty would result in another Anglo- Irish war which the I.R.A. would not be in a position to wage successfully, was bound to carry special conviction, given their intimate knowledge of the strengths and weaknesses of the forces they controlled. In the end, the alliance between these military deputies and moderate ones ensured the passage of the Treaty.[2]

Collins showed particular skill in making the military issue central to the debate. The overwhelming argument of the republican fundamentalist deputies was moral and metaphysical: that the Treaty was a betrayal of the republican ideal and a national humiliation. Supporters of the Treaty could not convincingly or successfully engage in a debate with this as a central theme. Instead, they concentrated on an argument they could win, focusing on the dangerous consequences of rejecting the British terms, and on the ultimate benefits likely to flow from the Treaty which, while clearly representing at least a temporary retreat from the republican demand, nevertheless left the way open for progressive advances along the road to a republic. This position, ultimately validated in the course of the following decade under the leadership of de Valera, the prime opponent of the settlement, was memorably expressed by Collins when he spoke of it as conferring on Irish people the freedom to achieve freedom.

Even following the intervention of the military deputies, the verdict of the Dáil might well have been otherwise. Some observers, including de Valera, believed that had a vote been taken before Christmas, the Treaty would have been rejected by a small majority. There is evidence that some deputies were influenced less by the issues under debate than by tactical blunders made on one side or the other, by personal loyalties and even by family heritage, as in the case of the relatives of such martyred patriots as Pearse, Thomas Clarke, Terence

MacSwiney and Michael O'Callaghan. De Valera gained no credit for his cause by submitting Document No. 2 to a Private Session and then insisting on withdrawing it. Bitter attacks on Collins's military capacity by Cathal Brugha and Seamus Robinson, the I.R.A. leader and Deputy for South Tipperary, led to some defections from the anti-Treaty side, while at least one deputy seems to have voted against the Treaty after the *Freeman's Journal* published a venomous leading article on de Valera for his "criminal attempt to divide the nation" and for not having "the instinct of an Irishman in his blood".

II

The Treaty debates brought to public notice the conflicts of personality and principle which had long been lurking under the surface of nationalist unity since October 1917 when de Valera, having ousted Griffith as President of Sinn Féin, had united people of widely differing political views including monarchists, moderate nationalists and republican separatists, in a single party whose official and somewhat pragmatic aim was to secure an Irish Republic which, according to de Valera, might be disestablished once secured if the Irish people desired this. The plenipotentiaries chosen by de Valera to negotiate the Treaty with Britain, knew, as de Valera did, that the unconditional recognition by Britain of an Irish republic was not going to be an outcome of the negotiations and at least one of them, Griffith, who favoured a dual monarchy, did not particularly desire that it should. Late in October 1921, it became evident to Griffith that the British would not, perhaps could not, agree to an Irish settlement that would exclude the monarch. On 24 October Griffith wrote to de Valera about the possible role of King George V in Irish affairs, a subject on which de Valera had given the plenipotentiaries no specific instructions. If the Irish negotiators came to an agreement on all other points, Griffith suggested to de Valera, he could recommend some form of association with the Crown. In reply, de Valera peremptorily rejected this course, warning the plenipotentiaries that the Irish people could not possibly be asked to enter an arrangement which would make them subject to the Crown, and the British side would have to be made to realise this. These comments angered Griffith and Collins, who pointed out that any form of association necessitated recognition in some form or another of the head of the association.

Similar conflicts involving de Valera and some members of his Cabinet on the one hand, and Collins and Griffith on the other, surfaced again at the beginning of December as the Treaty negotiations drew to a close. The weekend before the signing of the Treaty saw the visit of the plenipotentiaries to Dublin and their involvement in a Cabinet meeting at the Mansion House lasting from 11 a.m. to 7 p.m. on Saturday 3 December. The boat bringing Collins, Gavan Duffy and Childers had collided with a schooner on the way from Liverpool. They were a tired and haggard group when they reached the Mansion House. The Cabinet meeting was ragged, confusing and bitter. When it ended with the hurried departure of the plenipotentiaries for London, there was confusion among them about the mandate they had from the Cabinet. The meeting produced no agreed document to set against the British draft Treaty. The division of opinion among the plenipotentiaries was now clear. The split in the delegation was inspired to a large extent by the dominant position assumed by Collins and Griffith in the negotiations with the British: Barton, Gavan Duffy and Childers were largely excluded from the "confidential" discussions which took the form of sub-conferences attended only by Collins, Griffith and British Cabinet ministers. Even at an early stage Collins and Griffith made common cause with the British negotiators against the other members of the Irish delegation, particularly Childers, one of its secretaries who was regarded as de Valera's agent in London by those anxious to deprive him of an influential role.

On 26 October, Tom Jones, the British Cabinet Secretary, considered it important that the next British Document "should be shown in advance to Griffith and Collins so as to secure as much agreement as possible before it gets into the hands of Childers". Collins described the inspiration of Childers as "like farmland under water—dead". This animosity found expression during the Treaty debates in Griffith's reference to Childers as a "damned Englishman", and later still in suggestions made in the Dáil in the Spring of 1922 that he was a British spy.

A major issue of contention during the Treaty debates, and for long afterwards, was whether the plenipotentiaries had exceeded their powers by signing the Treaty without consulting Dublin first. Contemporary accounts of the Cabinet meeting of 3 December support the view that Griffith, in deference to the concerns expressed by de Valera and Cathal Brugha, agreed not to sign the British draft Treaty without referring it back to the Dáil. During the Private Session of the Dáil on 4 December, Griffith told an anti-Treaty deputy that he had given an undertaking to de Valera and Brugha that he would not sign the British draft Treaty he had brought with him from London on 3 December and that before signing anything, presumably a more acceptable version of this, he would try to get back to the Dáil. The Treaty signed on 6 December was an advance on the draft shown to the Cabinet meeting, but not the one de Valera wanted. In his diary entry on Griffith's death for 14 August 1922, de Valera asked rhetorically: "Did he [Griffith] think when he signed I'd accept the *fait accompli*?" In de Valera's eyes, the plenipotentiaries had offended, not only by signing a treaty without first consulting him, but by signing the Treaty they did. He was in Limerick when he heard that the Treaty had been signed, and assumed that External Association with the Empire, the position he favoured, had been conceded. The truth, when it was conveyed to him, shocked him profoundly. His Personal Secretary Kathleen O'Connell describes his response in her diary for 7 December:

> Treaty published in all the papers this morning. President in an awful state. Oh! What a disappointment to our

bright hopes—what a fiasco. Cabinet meeting at 11.30.
President was thinking of recalling Delegation, and asking
for resignation of Cabinet Ministers—Griffith, Collins and
Barton. Griffith's statement about "Freedom" such a farce.
Partition of our country and British subjects is the "freedom"
we are to have.

The Treaty debates are remarkable for the failure of the great
majority of the deputies to address the implications of the
settlement for the six north-eastern counties. The requirement
of an oath of loyalty to the British monarch seemed an
altogether more pressing burden than the imposition of a
permanent partition of the country which the implementation
of Articles 11 and 12 would inevitably involve. Sean Mac Entee
and Eoin O'Duffy, who represented border constituencies,
were the only deputies to recognise that partition as a *fait
accompli* was a much graver consequence of the Treaty than
the largely symbolic survival of the British monarchy in Irish
affairs. It is tempting to explain the general reluctance to
confront partition by invoking Article 12 of the Treaty, with its
proposal of a Boundary Commission which, Collins and
Griffith believed, might have so reduced the territory of the
six-county state as to make Irish unity inevitable.

III

One of the valuable aspects of *Free State or Republic?* is the light
it throws on the quality of de Valera's contribution to the
Treaty debates during which he was the dominant figure.
Those who judge this contribution purely on the evidence of
the published account of the proceedings tend to comment
unfavourably on the lack of balance and consistency evident
in his performance as a whole. Desmond Ryan, an objective
commentator, judged him a strange figure, "by turns formal-
istic and fiery, by turns passionate and dignified, by turns
personal and remote, by turns niggling on details and appealing

to his sacred principles". If one were to judge purely on the evidence of the published record, the general level of his contributions was poor. He is often negative, repetitious and tedious, and seems to lose the train of his thought. He is most reluctant to adhere to the set procedures of debate, making numerous interruptions, behaving like a querulous schoolmaster, correcting and admonishing his errant colleagues at every turn. He wants to have the first word and the last one. He introduces one long speech at the beginning of the debates by suggesting that it would be wise to give a short narrative of the circumstances under which the plenipotentiaries were approved. The number of pages in the record taken up by his speeches is almost double the combined total for Collins and Griffith. At many points, under the stress of emotion, he passes the boundaries of coherence and even common sense. When he is made angry by charges of inconsistency on the Republican issue, his self-defensive rhetoric merely confuses matters further in a welter of contradictory statements. There are times when even patient scrutiny of the text fails to yield satisfactory sense:

> As I said until the differences in the Cabinet arose when a break—off didn't occur on the matter of insisting on the question of allegiance, I would have faced the possibility of war with all that I know it means.

There are many possible interpretations of de Valera's tortuous, ambiguous use of language during the Treaty debates. It may have been that his intense, emotional involvement in the main issues led to sporadic loss of intellectual control, or that his command of the spoken language was inadequate to allow him to give proper expression to the complexities of his position. On the other hand, he may have sensed that his immediate purposes required nebulous or opaque formulations on which it would subsequently be difficult to pin him down. He certainly possessed a talent for using words to conceal, as well as to reveal, meaning. Akenson speaks of his ability "to obscure issues behind rhetoric not heard in the British Isles since the passing of Gladstone". Eamonn Duggan put the matter more bluntly in a frustrated comment in the course of the Treaty debates: "Now the President, when he gets up and makes ones of his impassioned and eloquent speeches, creates a kind of smoke-screen of words, so that it is almost impossible to see out of it into the world of fact."

The other, more favourable, side of de Valera's contribution to the Treaty debates is recorded by de Burca and Boyle, whose book is based on the daily reports they wrote for the *Irish Independent*. They gave due allowance to the many dreary, wearisome elements in the debate, the besetting sins of repetition and irrelevancy. At the same time, their response to de Valera's more effective interventions suggests that his listeners were vastly more impressed than one might have suspected. These comments usefully illustrate the contrast between the impression conveyed by the printed page and the effects of de Valera's speeches on an audience. No reader of the Treaty debates would suspect, for example, that de Valera's proposal on 19 December for the rejection of the Treaty "electrified the assembly", that his "blinding sincerity" left his listeners "dazzled and profoundly moved", that his "great speech, spoken straight from the heart of the man" earned a prolonged outburst of applause.

IV

Enquiries about the identity of John F. Boyle have so far proved fruitless. The life of his co-author, Padraig de Burca is, however, well documented.[3]

Born in Tipperary town in 1893, the son of a journalist who championed the cause of evicted tenants, de Burca took a B.A. in journalism at University College Cork, and was possibly the first to graduate in journalism at an Irish university. Between 1913 and 1919, he was a Secondary Teacher at Kells C.B.S. There he became involved with Sinn Féin, the I.R.B., the Gaelic League and the G.A.A. Between 1919 and 1960, he worked for the *Irish Independent*, where he became Chief Leader Writer and Literary Editor. In 1931 he was called to the Irish Bar, became a Senior Counsel in 1950, and was elected a Bencher of the King's Inns, Dublin in the 1960s. He was recognised in the Law Library as an expert in the law of landlord and tenant and the law of defamation. He died in 1975.

His involvement in the G.A.A. was lifelong. He played hurling and football with Meath, was a member of the Leinster Council of the G.A.A., legal adviser to the Association and a regular attender at its annual conference.

De Burca was a supporter of the Anglo-Irish Treaty, blaming de Valera for fomenting civil war. He was not, however, unreasonably partisan. In 1945, when de Valera earned universal public approval for his celebrated radio reply to Churchill's intemperate remarks on Irish neutrality, de Burca, believing that the *Irish Independent* should reflect the national mood, persuaded the editor that de Valera's speech should be acclaimed in a leading article which he himself wrote.

1 P. S. O'Hegarty, *The Victory of Sinn Féin* (Dublin, 1924, reprinted 1998), p. 54.
2 For a valuable account of these matters, see J. M. Regan, 'The politics of reaction; the dynamics of treatyite government and policy, 1922–33', *Irish Historical Studies*, November 1997, pp. 542–63.
3 De Burca's son, Marcus Bourke, a distinguished journalist, lawyer, editor and historian, has kindly provided details of his father's career.

FREE STATE
OR REPUBLIC?

PEN PICTURES OF THE HISTORIC
TREATY SESSION OF DÁIL ÉIREANN

BY

Padraig de Burca ("P. de B.")
and John F. Boyle

DUBLIN
THE TALBOT PRESS LIMITED
LONDON
T. FISHER UNWIN LIMITED
1922

PREFACE

THROUGH the courtesy of *Independent* Newspapers, Ltd., we are enabled to publish in book form our pen-pictures of the fateful session of Dáil Éireann to discuss the Peace Treaty with England. These articles originally appeared in the *Irish Independent*. To those who cannot find leisure to read through the wearisome debates the series should form a brief memento of the historic occasion, while preserving for posterity many of the touching incidents which are no less deserving of record. Written, as these articles were, while the proceedings were yet in progress, they suffer from all the shortcomings that must always be connected with such work for the Daily Press. However, we have made only the minimum of alterations necessary to make the book a connected whole. In order to complete the survey of the great events of the period, we have included our articles describing the meeting of the Ard-Comhairle of Sinn Fein and also the short session which formally ratified the Treaty. As an appendix we give the memorable Division List.

March, 1922.

FREE STATE OR REPUBLIC.

CHAPTER I.

AN DAIL ASSEMBLES.

DECEMBER 14TH, 1921

Two spacious rooms, low-ceilinged, opened into one by folding-doors. An array of small tables covered with pink cloth in one room. Row after row of plain college desks in the other. A dais with a carved arm-chair and oblong table in the centre. This was the simple setting for to-day's historic meeting of Dail Eireann assembled in University College, Dublin, to decide whether the Treaty of Peace with Great Britain shall or shall not be ratified.

At half-past ten the room in which the Deputies were to seat themselves was almost empty.

Mr. Eoin MacNeill, the Speaker, came in and went out at frequent intervals. He looked thinner, even, than of yore, but he was unexcited. Sean T. O'Kelly, back from Paris, was also in and out several times. He was active, in a calm and unemotional manner. Mr. Robert Barton, neatly dressed as usual, sat near a window, thoughtful and motionless.

At 11 a.m. there were not six Deputies in this room. Yet there was incessant movement in the other one. A battalion of Pressmen—and Presswomen—had assembled. Restricted to space, they were crowded like sardines. They represented newspapers in every civilised portion of the globe. Through them news of the meeting was flashed to the ends of the earth.

Shortly after 11 the Deputies filed in. They seated themselves quietly. One T.D. was in the uniform of an officer. Most of them were dressed in black, or in grey tweed. Dr. White, of Waterford, wore a frock coat. All eyes turned involuntarily to the leaders in front of the Speaker's chair. On the left-hand side sat Eamon de Valera. With him were Austin Stack and Cathal Brugha. From a medium-sized attache case Eamon de Valera took a bundle of papers and laid them on the half-moon table at which he sat. Then he conversed for some minutes with Austin Stack.

The latter's face was grim, fixed and stern. On the other hand, de Valera, though he looked grave, did not seem preoccupied, nor did he present an unbending appearance. Three slips of paper, bound with a fastener, he held loosely.

On the right-hand side of the Speaker sat Arthur Griffith, and next to him Michael Collins. Ordinarily pale, Griffith now looked a little flushed. Otherwise he wore that impassive, reflective, unshakeable look of his that those of us who knew him in the old days used to remark so minutely. Michael Collins and he chatted together, but not animatedly.

All stood. The Chaplain said prayers in Irish. Roll-call in Gaelic followed. The next business was the Private Session motion. Before it was mentioned Eamon de Valera was on his feet. He spoke in Irish. Then slowly, and almost conversationally, he drifted into English. His voice seemed almost casual—there was absolutely no effort at tense and emotional eloquence. His left hand lay by his side. His right hand held the three typewritten slips of paper.

He was speaking of the instructions given to the Pleni-potentiaries. The division in the Cabinet was nothing dramatic—nothing extraordinary. As he spoke in this strain I saw Arthur Griffith nod his head as if in approval.

But when de Valera went on to allude to instructions, to Cabinet policy, to final texts, to the signing of the Treaty, then Collins and Griffith compared papers together. The feeling of tension in the rapt audience that hung on every word began to rise.

Had or had not the Plenipotentiaries exceeded their instructions ? Eamon de Valera read out Paragraph 3 of the instructions given to them in writing. He did not emphasise his points unduly, but he said the directions in this paragraph had not been carried out.

Michael Collins rose to his feet. In repose his eyes glimmer softly and with humour. When aroused they narrow—hard, intense and relentless. He speaks like this. One or two words. Then he pauses to think. His speech does not flow like a stream as it does in the case of Eamon de Valera. Yet not from one word is firmness absent. The issue had taken an unfair aspect. Instructions had been read but not all the instructions. " The thing that matters now," he said, " is that I am against a private session." That set the discussion right ahead on Order 2 of the agenda.

Dr. White proposed his motion. The arguments he and other speakers used were that the Deputies could talk more freely in private than in public session. It was soon clear that this view only found partial acceptance. Richard Mulcahy favoured a private discussion first and then a public session after.

Leaping to his feet, Eamon de Valera agreed.

" The big question is a matter for the whole nation." Deputies throbbed in sympathy.

One after another they arose in quick succession. Clean-shaven, resolute faces   Only military and financial matters should be discussed in private—" unknown to the enemy," said one Deputy to whom the Enemy was The Enemy still.

Once again Michael Collins was speaking. With hands in pockets he faced the chair, and his words came slowly but never, for one instant, haltingly. He entered a protest

A document had been read—not all the documents. " Read the original document served on each member of the Delegation," he said in a voice vibrant with the intensity of his feelings.

Eamon de Valera stood up. They faced one another across the table. It was a dramatic moment. But it was only a moment. Michael Collins turned to the Speaker. " I think," he said, calmly, and almost jocosely, " that I have the right to speak without interruption." He halted for a moment before saying it. He had not yet mastered the art of gripping an assembly like this. It came easier to Eamon de Valera.

The little incident ended in a ripple of relaxation and some applause. De Valera sat down. Collins went on with his speech. With dramatic effect he read the original credentials, signed by Eamon de Valera, and dated and sealed October 7th, 1921. The words " negotiate and conclude " occur here. He did not stress them, yet the reading of these sweeping instructions created a profound impression.

From slow, measured tones his speech mounted until it reached a crescendo of anger and indignation.

" I have not said a harsh word about anybody, but I have been called a traitor. Well, let the Irish people decide whether I am or not."

As he spoke, passionately and earnestly, he rapped the table in front with his right hand.

De Valera, with lightning rapidity, jerked out the words,

" By whom ? " Collins continued speaking. The Deputies were listening with tense anxiety. " If there are men who call me traitor I am ready to meet them anywhere, any time, now, as in the past." It was a challenge—not uttered with provocative emphasis, but with deep feeling. There were slight murmurs. De Valera was staring in front of him, a slight frown on his face. Griffith wore his inscrutable look that told nothing. Ministers and Deputies became a little restless. Then with astounding rapidity the mercury fell.

In almost ordinary tones, but with the emphatic note never absent, Michael Collins placed his cards on the table. " Ireland has full liberty to accept or reject. I signed and I recommend. That is all. If the Dail does not accept, I am relieved of all responsibility. I fall into the ranks."

The words had a soothing effect.

De Valera followed. The main point was settled. It would be ridiculous to think that five men could complete a Treaty without the Dail's ratification. This Treaty might bind Ireland for centuries. De Valera's tone was conciliatory, if argumentative. The debate drifted. A Deputy : " Let us begin with a private session." The proposal finds favour.

For a time attention flags. Deputies speak for and against. Suddenly we are back again on the powers of the Plenipotentiaries. Cathal Brugha had spoken in Irish. Only a few words. Eamon de Valera listened, with his hands deep in his pockets. The debate still seems to hang on the private session motion. But no. De Valera rises to his feet, and his compelling power diverts at once attention from the prosaic motion. Griffith and Collins are chatting earnestly. Madame Markievicz has removed her hat and scarf and sits jauntily confident. Ministers

and Deputies are looking this way and that. De Valera
flings out his question :—

" Do you wish to lay stress on the word ' conclude ' ? "
Collins looks up and replies quietly and promptly, " No,
sir, no." De Valera dots the i's and crosses the t's. " It
was never intended that Plenipotentiaries should bind this
nation by their signatures."

No one rose to dispute this assertion. Eamon de Valera
went on to dwell on technicalities—the technical point
of view in relation to the word " conclude." Like the
ebb and flow of the tide the debate softened and receded.

The Speaker was discussing the private session motion
and was making a suggestion, when Arthur Griffith arose.

" Whether we had full power to make this Treaty
binding on this nation is a question that never arose."

Deputies sensed the underlying meaning of this momentous phrase, and there was relieved applause. One felt
that they were glad at being thus told so bluntly by the
Chairman of the Delegation of Plenipotentiaries that they
had the fullest and most perfect freedom of action in the
discussion over Ratification. Eamon de Valera for the
first time smiled—not a mocking or an ironical smile but
one that illumined his grave and austere features. Mr.
Gavan Duffy stood up. " I have kept silence," he said,
" but I must say, and I will say, what I have to say in
public."

It was the final personal touch in the public proceedings.
For the last time the debate turned on the private session
motion, and it stood there until that issue was decided.
" The Irish people are our masters," said one speaker.
Agreed. With arms folded, de Valera sat motionless.
Austin Stack and Cathal Brugha were sphinx-like at his
side On the opposite side Griffith and Collins sat with
set faces, whilst Lord Mayor O'Callaghan, William

Cosgrave, Liam de Roiste, and Joseph MacDonagh spoke.

A model of precision, and a lover of order in debate, it remained for Deputy Cosgrave to call attention in a friendly way to the rule of debate. Members could not speak more than once. As a matter of fact, Eamon de Valera spoke six times, Michael Collins three times, and Arthur Griffith, Austin Stack, Cathal Brugha, Richard Mulcahy, Gavan Duffy only once each. Mr. Etchingham spoke a couple of times.

Finally, on the motion of Eamon de Valera, seconded by Michael Collins, the House went into Secret Session for the day, and the small army corps of Pressmen trooped out like college boys into the corridors of the new University.

J. F. B.

CHAPTER II.

THE TREATY MOVED.

DECEMBER 19TH, 1921.

THE sun shone brightly through the windows of University College. It was an omen of cheer to the Deputies. They assembled in pleasant humour. I saw them smiling and beaming as they gathered in the lobby. That air of tense absorption apparent on the opening day was absent. They understood better exactly where they were after three full days of Secret Session. Madame Markievicz, in a white blouse and a black fur, shook hands with the visitors on the front bench. Then a roar of cheering came from outside. The leaders were arriving. Soon they were in the room. Eamon de Valera perused a foolscap sheet of paper attentively. Mr. Arthur Griffith walked to his seat on the right of the Speaker with that air of detachment so characteristic of him.

The members formed into little groups. One of the lady members in deep black approached Mr. Michael Collins and spoke to him. There is great activity. Secretaries to Ministers enter with bundles of papers.

Messrs. Eamon de Valera, Austin Stack, and Erskine Childers are seated together. Mr. de Valera, with his hand to his mouth, looks absorbed. The Minister for Home Affairs wears that stern look which rarely leaves his face. Erskine Childers is reflective in that pale, rather white, and keenly cold way of his. Sean T. Kelly moves about, busy and very active. Several members are reading documents and papers. Others are buried in thought. The ladies, in deep black, seem sombre. Michael Collins, clean-shaven, looks perfectly fit and in perfect humour. Mr. Duggan and Mr. Griffith are chatting. Richard Mulcahy reads from a weighty document.

It is an interesting scene, abounding in remarkable personalities. A touch of colour is lent by the appearance of Deputies in I.R.A. uniform. William T. Cosgrave sits behind Mr. de Valera and his colleagues. Near him is Joseph MacDonagh, looking cheerful and fatter but very inscrutable. Mrs. Pearse, Mrs. Clarke, Miss MacSwiney, and Madame Markievicz are all in the centre. Thus it is when roll-call takes place.

Immediately developments arise. It occurs over a document—over a document that is to become famous in the history of Ireland. The personal interest lies in the fact that Eamon de Valera and Arthur Griffith are on their feet facing one another in front of the Speaker. The question is, shall the contents of this document be published ? I pass over the incident now because it ended (for the moment) almost as quickly as it began. It leaves both Griffith and de Valera rather pale, and every listener thrills in sympathy. The December sun sends its gleams into the Chamber, and the electric atmosphere is dissolved. But we shall hear more of that Document.

Arthur Griffith rises to move the Ratification of the Treaty. His speech speaks for itself. I shall not touch on many of its points here. Rather do I chose to dwell on its manner of delivery. It was a speech prepared with great care, thought over deeply, and delivered with intense earnestness. As is his habit, he began and concluded in the same key. He never varied.

I watched Mr. Griffith carefully, minutely, during the

entire delivery. At times he bent towards the Deputies in order to emphasise a sentence or a paragraph. He took up his typewritten slips. He laid them down. He placed his hands at the sides of his waistcoat. He stroked his tie. He laid more stress on some words rather than others. But he never strove to be eloquent. Rather did he seem to be an advocate striving to appeal to the reason of his hearers.

Some allusions struck the brain and were focussed there. This Treaty has been examined with a microscope —or words to that effect. " We are here—not as dictators, but as representatives of the Irish people." And so on. There was not a trace of hesitation—of halting, of desire to shirk awkward words such as the " British Empire."

As Griffith spoke de Valera was very busy with his papers. " By that Treaty I am going to stand." Griffith spoke the words firmly.

I notice Mrs. Pearse as Arthur Griffith spoke. She was listening with calm intensity and she followed every succeeding speaker with the same interest. Mrs. O'Callaghan sat near her, and her features reflected no emotions that I could detect, save sadness. It was impossible also to detect the feelings of Ministers. Erskine Childers seemed always to be melancholy.

The voice of Griffith became more clear and resonant as he proceeded. One point he hammered home mercilessly. The issue was not between an independent Republic and Dominion status. Rather was it between two forms of Association with the British Empire. He alluded to that Document again—Document No. 2—and held that his hands were tied by its non-publication. We gathered that he was referring to something produced at the Secret Session and we were puzzled for the moment. But the phrasing of his speech never altered. There was no emotional reaction after the applause. The one change was the quiet peroration—a quotation from Davis—Thomas Davis, the poet and Young Ireland patriot, whose works Griffith has edited.

Then a surprise followed. From the left-hand side of the hall near the end stood Commandant Sean McKeon to second the Ratification. The famous blacksmith of Ballinalee drew all eyes as he began to speak.

Clean-shaven, sturdily-built, wearing a soft collar, his pure, rich voice sounded like a whiff of fresh country air through the assembly. His hands were sunk in the pockets of his plain tweed suit. A man of action, he is not an orator, and he halted more than once. But some of his sayings remained in the mind after he sat down. What he wanted—what the Irish people wanted—was not shadows but substance. He was an extremist—but that meant he had an extreme love of his country. The words evoked heartfelt cheers.

It was then that Eamon de Valera arose. He was in magnificent form—mentally and physically. Unquestionably his speech electrified the assembly. His blinding sincerity so impresses you that you find yourself listening dazzled and profoundly moved. Every word came with rugged clearness. Here, too, was no faltering or no hesitation.

Like every other leader in Dail Eireann, he has the faculty in excellence of going direct, straight ahead, to the heart of the subject. " Did the Irish people think we were liars." Hands at side, he stood tall, erect, straight, fearless. " I am against this Treaty because it will not bring peace with England. It will not even bring peace in Ireland." He rapped the table to press every word home.

It was while Eamon de Valera was speaking that I noticed the applause. It was distinct both in the case of Griffith and of de Valera. He would be a wise man who could deduce from its volume the support behind either. Many Deputies did not cheer at all. That is a simple fact. I watched, and I saw that. As Mr. de Valera went on to speak of the King of England and of black flags in the streets of Dublin if he came over to Ireland, Eamon de Valera placed one hand in his pocket, and spoke with passionate feeling. " Would that make for harmony between the peoples ? " What they wanted was a peace of peoples !

With both hands stretched towards the Assembly, he told why he opposed the Treaty. " It does not do the fundamental thing. It does not bring us peace." Just as Griffith quoted Davis, so, too, did de Valera quote Parnell.

For one dramatic instant he pointed his right hand at Arthur Griffith. " Time will tell," he declared propheti-cally, " time would tell, if this Treaty were ratified, whether it would be a final settlement. You are presuming to set bounds to the onward march of a nation." With these words directed to the supporters of the Treaty, he sat down. There was a prolonged outburst of applause as his last words were slowly and impressively uttered. It was a great speech, spoken straight from the heart of the man.

Austin Stack got up. He neither aims at emotional power or at cheer getting. He reminds me of Ceannt. His whole face is that of a speaker of unbending firmness. He analysed the clauses in a sharp and businesslike way. " I stand for full independence, and nothing short of it." Here was an uncompromising utterance, spoken with stern strength.

His words came slowly, distinctly, unmistakeably. Like Mr. de Valera, he rapped on the half-moon table occasionally to lend additional strength to his words. His chief sat beside him listening thoughtfully.

Speaking in a low voice, Count Plunkett (the father of one of the executed leaders of Easter Week) followed. As he proceeded his voice grew stronger. In feeling terms he referred to his boys (one dead and the other transported for their love of Ireland). The whole assembly was moved to sympathy. He meant to be faithful to his oath as he was faithful to the dead.

He had scarcely resumed his seat when Joseph MacBride rose to support the Treaty. Just as Count Plunkett had lost a son so Joseph MacBride had lost a brother (Major MacBride) in 1916. Yet here they were on opposite sides in regard to this Treaty. The contrast struck everyone.

Joseph MacBride is grey like Count Plunkett, but here the resemblance ends. The latter is tall and stately. The former is smaller in stature, florid, and rather stout. He spoke very briefly. " I will vote for the Treaty," he said, " because I believe it will serve the best interests of the country."

When the Dail reassembled at half-past three the lights were on, and a dark December evening had begun. Michael Collins was on his feet in an instant and plunged right ahead into his speech in support of this Treaty.

Amongst the group of people at the back of the battalion of Pressmen were a Japanese and a tall negro. Both craned their necks to see the redoutable Michael Collins. He spoke passionately, eagerly, pervadingly. He had his manuscript before him. He rarely consulted it. He preferred to rely on his intuition—on the unfailing native power of the Irishman to move, rouse and convince his hearers.

Now and again he felt his smooth chin. He tossed his

thick black hair with his hands. He rummaged among his documents. Like Mr. de Valera, he stands now upright, now bent, now calm, and now quivering with emotion.

On a previous occasion I said Michael Collins spoke slowly. He does—until he is aroused. Then the words come in a ceaseless stream. Yesterday his speech was devoted to a prolonged and emphatic defence of the Treaty, section by section.

In the middle of it there was an interlude. Michael Collins made an allusion to the Coalition—opposite him. The Coalition of External Associationists and out-and-out isolated Republicans ! There was silence for a moment, and then a roar of laughter. I never saw Mr. de Valera laugh more heartily or more unrestrainedly. It was a wonderful relief—this glimmer of humour into a tense debate.

For the first time, also, Michael Collins struck another new note He alluded to Ulster. I took it that his plea was the possibility of the North coming in with good-will under the Treaty.

Then he spoke some plain words to the Irish-Americans. If they wanted to help them let them send men and rifles as well as dollars. From beginning to end of his speech no responsibility was shirked. " I speak plainly," he said. He did.

A thin, slight figure arose. It was Erskine Childers. Every line of his face is illumined by the pale cast of thought. His speech was one long, devastating criticism of the Treaty, word by word, clause by clause. One felt he was not merely condemning it to death—he was dissecting it as well.

Kevin O'Higgins took the opposite line. His first words were directed to the speech of Erskine Childers. " Mr.

Childers has told us what is wrong with it. He did not tell us how we were to better the Treaty." From this Kevin O'Higgins went on to refer to the Cabinet, and this drew a strong but temperate objection from Mr. de Valera. " Cabinet discussions should not be divulged." The incident passed.

Sean MacSwiney, a young Deputy in the body of the hall, speaking in low but vibrant tones, went against the Treaty, and referred to the feelings of the army in Munster about it. He could speak for the army in Munster.

This paved the way for one of the four remarkable speeches of the day—that of Robert Barton. With an accent like that of Erskine Childers, he told a hushed and expectant House how he came to sign the Treaty. It was not free choice—there was a terrible alternative. The issue was—peace or war. They had to accept or reject. For himself, he preferred war ; but with three members of the Delegation ready to sign, what was he to do ?

This snapshot does not even skim the lines of his remarkable speech. It had a dramatic effect. Every listener drew a long breath—and pondered.

And it was thus when the sitting adjourned till eleven o'clock next morning.

J. F. B.

CHAPTER III.

LADY CREATES A SCENE.

WHEN we took our seats in the Council Chamber this morning there was little to indicate the seriousness of the great drama that was being staged.

At 11 o'clock the Chamber was almost empty. Eamon de Valera sat alone at his table absorbed in his notes, while Michael Collins, Gavan Duffy, and Sean Milroy appeared in the room only to leave almost as soon.

A few minutes after the appointed hour Erskine Childers, looking more than usually melancholy, entered and took his place beside his chief. Padraig O'Maille, appearing perfectly at his ease, was enjoying a smoke in a back bench. Seamus Robinson was industriously compiling notes under the Speaker's chair, while Madame Markievicz was conning her sheaf of notes as if to assure herself they were invincible.

It was half-an-hour after the appointed time when the main body of the Teachtai trooped into their places. It was curious to note how even already each member goes to the seat which he occupied at the first public session.

After ten minutes had been spent in preliminary explanations Sean Etchingham arose to demolish the case for Ratification. His speech was a blend of the humorous and the melodramatic, delivered in a tone curiously reminiscent of a veteran preacher. " Our people have been

16

stampeded," he declared, and in denouncing the proposed
oath of allegiance he travelled from Webster's Dictionary
to the Apocalypse which, curiously enough, he referred
to as the Book of Revelation.   His arguments would,
perhaps, have been more telling had he been briefer.

Fionan Lynch, with fire flashing from his eyes, and with
a grim look on his ruddy countenance, and speaking
with a clear, ringing voice, held the floor for 18 minutes.
" The bones of the dead have been rattled indecently in
the face of this Assembly," he declared.   Then he went
on to give the Dail his arguments for Ratification.

" I can," he proceeded, " speak for the people of
South Kerry—— "

" No ! "

The House was thunderstruck.   The dissenting voice
was that of a sombre lady sitting in the body of the hall.
All eyes were turned upon her, and Fionan Lynch, with
biting emphasis, completed his sentence——

" With one exception—an Englishwoman."

The interrupter was asked to leave the Chamber.
Quietly closing her notebook, and still smiling, the
Honourable Albinia Broderick, Republican sister of a
Southern Unionist Peer, left the hall.

The speech of Mrs. O'Callaghan, widow of the murdered
Mayor of Limerick, was a vindication of feminine intel-
lectualism and a defence of the name of her dead husband.
She spoke in a clear, cultured voice, with her emphasis
magnificently placed, and without having once to pause
for a word.   She held a bundle of notes in her hand but
rarely consulted them in making her case against the
Treaty.

Once, indeed, she drew a broad smile from the usually
stern countenance of Mr. de Valera when she said she
knew many members who were neither legal nor logical.

It would scarcely be necessary to be told that Mr. Hogan, who spoke in defence of the Treaty, had been bred to the legal profession. He held his sheaf of notes in his left hand just as if it had been a brief, and he paused with that regularity which men who have dealings with unskilled magistrates always find essential.

His assertion that the Treaty gives us the right to have our own coastal defences after five years was received with a storm of dissent, led, I think, by Mr. de Valera, whose emphatic, " No ! " was repelled from the other side by a no less emphatic " Yes ! " from Mr. Collins. Then Mr. Hogan gave us the actual words of the Treaty. And both sides were right.

Ald. Sean T. O'Kelly was the last speaker before the adjournment.

"Ḃ'ḟeaṙṙ liom" an ṙeiṙeaṅ, "Laḃaiṙc an faṫ aṙ Ġaeḋilg, aċ ceiṙc caḃaċcaċ í ṙeo, aguṙ ó'ṙ ṙuḋ guṙ ḟeaṙṙ a cuiġṗeaṅ aṙ Ḃéaṙla í ḃ'ḟeaṙṙ an ceiṙc a ṗléiḋe aṙ Ḃéaṙla, maṙ iṙ eól ḋuinn go léiṙ ná ḟuil in a láṅ ḋinn aċ coṙnuiġceóiṙí ná ṙeaḋṙaḋ a ṙmaoince ḋo noċcaḋ aṙ Ġaeḋilg."

His was the first reference to Sinn Fein. The oath which the members of the Free State Parliament were asked to take was a violation of the Sinn Fein Constitution. Unlike most of the previous speakers, he relied mainly on his notes.

The motion for the private session introduced the first unpleasant note to the day's proceedings.

The opposition to that motion suggested to Mr. de Valera that " something else besides a Treaty has come from Downing St." The sentence was unworthy of de Valera ; but he made the *amende honorable* in the afternoon, when his generous apology was a happy augury to what proved to be the liveliest sitting we have yet had.

Sean Milroy treated the House to a fifty minutes' oration, the longest yet delivered in the public session. He spoke with a deep, sonorous voice, rolling his r's and vigorously driving home his thrusts by the scornful finger he pointed at the Cabinet minority, and the resounding bang with which he brought his clenched fist down on the table.

His speech was brimful of sarcasm and incision. It was unquestionably the ablest speech of the day on the side of the Ratifiers. " Is this country to be driven to war for a shadow ? " he asked.

With the skill of an old acquaintance of the public platform, again and again he hurled back the grenades of his opponents into their own ranks. In a less harmonious assembly his opponents would have curled up before his lash of invective ; but the members of Dail Eireann are of a different mould. The picture of Cathal Brugha as the Napoleon leading an expedition against the Isle of Man convulsed the Assembly, but none laughed more heartily than the Minister of Defence himself.

Alderman MacDonagh was a vigorous opponent of the Treaty. Neither Griffith nor Milroy was true to the stand he had once taken, and the Alderman quoted Mitchel with effect against the Minister for Foreign Affairs.

Dr. MacCartan's speech was the sensation of the day. With a sincerity that none of those who heard him could gainsay, he piled scorn and contumely on the heads of both sections of the Cabinet alike. He was still a doctrinaire Republican, but the Republic had been laid to rest by both parties. Whatever any other member might do, he at least was true to the Republic—a remark which won the unanimous applause of the lady deputies.

Before the adjournment we heard some straight talk from Michael Collins about punctuality. " Let eleven o'clock be eleven o'clock," said Michael in that way he has of saying things which only his audience can appreciate.

Irish journalists who have to take notes in the midst of an assembly of priests, professors and ladies, and who have no prescriptive right to any particular seat, heartily said amen to the prayer for punctuality.

P. DE B.

CHAPTER IV.

ALDERMAN COSGRAVE'S HUMOUR.

WEDNESDAY, DECEMBER 21ST, 1921.

THE hour to decide the fate of the Peace Treaty is drawing nigh, and but few of the great actors in the drama remain to appear before the footlights.

The common people will not be sorry when the end comes. They are aweary of all this discussion and of all this repetition. Day by day the group that faces University College grows thinner.

To-day, when we were entering, one impatient bystander who cannot be congratulated upon his acquaintance with the personnel of An Dail, impressed upon a group of journalists the view that they must ratify the Treaty !

The privileged ones who may enter the Council Chamber were not as numerous as on previous days. But the two coloured students were again in their places, and followed the debate with undivided attention.

Once more the boyish face of the maimed warrior, who was dressed in the uniform of a Republican officer, was turned to the Speaker's chair, while his crutches rested by his side. The University professor who abandoned his lecture hall in Cork to give what help he might to the Plenipotentiaries in London occupied his seat as on previous days.

The rebuke which Michael Collins administered to the unpunctual on Tuesday evening had its effect. Most of the deputies—it is strange they do not say Teachtai— were in their places at eleven o'clock.

Gavan Duffy's speech had been promised to us as a sensation. We were assured by those " in the know " that he was going to oppose the Treaty which he had signed. The sensation was not forthcoming.

His speech was brief, restrained, and businesslike. Speaking in a voice which was at times almost inaudible, he recommended the Treaty reluctantly but sincerely.

" My heart is with those who are against the Treaty, but my head is against them, for I can see no rational alternative." That was his case, and that was the challenge which drew from de Valera the emphatic " Yes "—there was a rational alternative.

We had been told, too, that Professor Stockley was amongst the doubtfuls. He spoke for twenty-five minutes, and at the end of that time we were still in doubt as to which side he would take, though the letter he read from Mrs. MacSwiney seemed to place him with de Valera.

He spoke in the manner of a judge summing up in a case where much has been said on both sides, and where the course of right was not clear. As Mr. Griffith's national hero is Thomas Davis, Professor Stockley left little doubt upon our minds that the political philsopher of his choosing is Edmund Burke, the mention of whose name seemed so little appropriate in a meeting of Dail Eireann. The excuse, we suppose, is to be found not in Professor Stockley's creed of nationality, but in his profession.

We were sorry that the Professor read that letter from the widow of Terence MacSwiney, declaring that her husband, if he were alive, would not have supported the Treaty. On Tuesday, when Fionan Lynch protested against the " rattling of the bones of the dead," the House cheered from all sides, and we thought there was an end of it. Unfortunately, however, many of the speakers on both sides have still insisted on disturbing the patriots' graves.

The reading of the letter drew from Michael Collins and Arthur Griffith another emphatic protest that they, too, could quote the dead and the widows of the dead.

A few minutes later Professor Stockley asked permission to read a further letter, but there was what appeared to be an unanimous " No," whereupon Professor Stockley convulsed the House by explaining that the letter was " entirely against himself ! "

Mr. Whelehan's best point was against Dr. MacCartan, who had declared that the Republic was dead, and that the alternative to the Treaty was chaos. Yet Dr. MacCartan is not going to vote. But, argued Mr. Whelehan, is not Dr. MacCartan, then, bound to vote for the Treaty to deliver the country from chaos ?

Mr. de Valera got angry during this speech. When Mr. Whelehan spoke of the powers they would have over education, de Valera cut in with scornful emphasis, " Yes, education based on dishonour." And he scowled with the contempt which only de Valera can scowl, and his head sunk upon the fingers of his left hand, and he brooded with the silence of a man whose dream has been shattered.

David Kent, who followed Mr. Whelehan, spoke with the rapidity which is the birthright of a Corkman. He was still a Republican, and his rugged countenance showed his sincerity better than his words could do.

Eamonn Duggan, the last of the Plenipotentiaries to address the House, was not wearisome. He spoke for twenty-two minutes. Sean Etchingham was his first victim, for " Lloyd George," he said, " shook no paper in my face."

It was time, too, that the note was struck in which he boldly told us there was no monopoly of patriotism on either side of the House. One looked instinctively from de Valera to Collins, from Austin Stack to Fionan Lynch, and from Cathal Brugha to Arthur Griffith.

Mr. Ruttledge, whose opposition to the Treaty was soon made clear, made an able, but over-long, contribution to the debate. The House has had enough, and more than enough, of declarations that we must stand upon principle. No matter what be our views regarding the Treaty, surely we must allow to both sides honesty and sincerity. What, then, is the purpose of any member declaring that he in particular stands for principle ?

The afternoon session again began sharp to time. It was noticed that before the debate was resumed an offical was busy delivering a huge bundle of telegrams, and at once we agreed—"The voice of the country—for or against ?"

Mr. Collins, too, made a much-needed suggestion when he urged that members who rose to speak should approach the Speaker's chair. One Deputy who contributed a quarter of an hour's speech since the public session opened —it is not necessary to mention his name—was not heard distinctly in a solitary sentence at some of the back seats reserved, or theoretically reserved, for the Press. Under such circumstances it is little wonder that members are misinterpreted.

It was good to be present at the afternoon sitting. Everybody was in the best of humour, for Ald. Cosgrave provided us with a delightful comic relief to the awful seriousness of the situation.

He began by tearing to shreds every argument which had been levelled at the proposed oath of allegiance. Then, notwithstanding the proximity of de Valera, he entered the realm of mathematics

" Now if x were absolute independence," said the mystified Alderman, " and y be the independence we are told we are abandoning, what is the relative value of x and y ? "

That was not altogether an indeterminate equation. But when the Minister for Local Government added forty million pounds to x and 60,000 British troops to y, even de Valera was dumbfounded. He sought inspiration by running his fingers through his hair, but 'twas vain. With a broad smile he gave it up with a despairing nod.

With the skill of an experienced debater Alderman Cosgrave hurled the arguments of the opposition back into their own camp. Continuing with the self-composure of an after-dinner speaker he won even the admiration of Mr. de Valera's supporters by the delightful irony with which he turned Mr. Childers' arguments on the Canadian Constitution back upon their author.

One would need to be present to appreciate the humour of the cross-fire between the Alderman and those around him.

" Even the President," he declared, " could bear witness to the fact that our best colleges play the foreign games." Mr. de Valera nodded his assent, and to many in the Chamber there came the picture of the de Valera of former days leading a Rockwell pack in a break from a scrum.

Alderman Cosgrave's, too, was the lot to strike the first note of appeal to " Ulster." And his retort to those who would say that the association of the Free State with the Empire meant responsibility for the oppression of India and Egypt brought an emphatic " hear, hear " from Michael Collins ; for is it not more probable, argued the speaker, that the Free State will then be in a stronger position to stand by these oppressed peoples ?

At 4.25 Miss MacSwiney arose. She concluded exactly

at 7 o'clock. She had then spoken against the Treaty for precisely the same length of time as the five Plenipotentiaries had taken with their combined speeches.

Not once during that time did she pause to cast more than a passing glance at her notes. Speaking with the clear musical ring which belongs only to a cultured Cork accent, she reviewed the whole history of the Republican movement and the inner history of the events that preceded the making of the Treaty.

At times the listener wondered whether she was the teacher or the disciple of Terence MacSwiney. Not that she once mentioned his name. She, at least, allowed the heroic dead to rest.

But ever and anon through her speech there burst forth those philosophic generalisations which one will for ever connect with the name of the Brixton martyr. "No physical victory can compensate for a spiritual surrender." . . . "This fight has been a spiritual fight."

Perhaps she was at times too severe. The sarcasm with which she referred to the "superior voice" of two members was unworthy of the speaker and the occasion.

P. DE B.

CHAPTER V.

A DAY OF FERVID ORATORY.

DEPUTIES are feeling the strain. There can be no doubt of that. Eight days of prolonged and animated debate have placed imprints on their faces. Eamon de Valera looked pale, thin, and rather gaunt as he took his seat this morning, and entered into a subdued conversation with Mrs. Clarke. Erskine Childers seemed even more gloomy than ever—if that were possible. Arthur Griffith sat quietly thoughtful in his corner, but he would not be human if he did not present the appearance of a man who has gone through not only an exacting week, but a terrible month. Michael Collins came in hurriedly, clad in a fawn overcoat, and placed his attache case with a bang on the table. The Assembly room was only half-filled when the sitting began. Those who were present had slightly bored expressions as the speakers rose to their feet.

First speaking in Irish, Professor Michael Hayes, of the National University, plunged at once into a rational defence of the Treaty. It was not an impressive speech, but it was an eminently commonsense one. A young man, stoutly built, with a black moustache, he spoke without the theatrical effects—so apparent in other orators—and argued that the Irish nation had never got as much re-cognition from the world as it had obtained in this Treaty

from Great Britain. He had scarcely sat down when
" Sceilg "—Deputy J. J. Kelly—stood bolt upright and
in a ringing speech opposed the Treaty. He does not use
many gestures. He speaks as a rule with his hands behind
his back. But not even de Valera denounces with more
violent force. It was by far the most passionate, fiery,
raging, rousing speech delivered against the Treaty. Yet
it evoked little applause. Burning the words came—red
hot—and still the jaded audience did not leap to their
feet cheering. Perhaps they were aweary of words.

It was to the oath of allegiance that " Sceilg " devoted
his most scornful invective. He, for one, had taken a
solemn oath to the Republic and he meant to keep that—
without equivocation. The most serious statement in his
speech was the declaration that if this pact were approved
it would mean war—and war in a divided Ireland. Now
and again " Sceilg's " voice sank to ordinary pitch. Then
it rose to a crescendo of rage and indignation and anger as
he tore the Treaty to shreds. At a public meeting it would
have aroused tornadoes of cheers. In Dail Eireann its
cadences sank and arose almost without interruptions.
Sean McKeon arose to point out in a manly voice that he
had seconded the adoption of the Treaty of his own free
will. Michael Collins, his voice quivering with resentment,
also took exception to some references to the Plenipotentiaries and, with the words flowing like lava from his throat,
said : " We are here to answer to a tribunal of the Irish
people. At least," he added pointedly, " some of us are."

" Sceilg " continued. To the very end he never varied
in his inflexible opposition to the Treaty. " Consign it
to oblivion," he said. Then he sat down calm and collected
after as vividly an impassioned utterance as I have ever
heard.

A stout, splendidly-built, clean-shaven, and impressive

figure follows. It is Padraig O'Maille. In sonorous tones
he rolls out his Irish sentences. The speech for a long time
continues in the language of the Gael. It is with regret
that he relapses into the English tongue. When he does
his powerful, mellow voice pervades every nook and corner
of the long, double room. " I support this Treaty," he
said, with profound emphasis, " because in my heart and
soul I believe it is best for Ireland."

It was a homely speech. Disregarding mere invective
he appealed to the plain, common man—that poor man in
the street or on the road about whom so much is heard,
but whose views are apparently regarded by some politicians with so little respect. As one listened to the rich
country accent and to the blunt practical opinions of
Padraig O'Maille it was like hearing a calm judge summing
up after an eloquent but entirely denunciatory counsel
had just finished.

Speaking in a low, a very low, tone, Mrs. Clarke opposed
the Treaty. A small, pathetic figure in deep black, she
spoke from notes in her hand, and her sombre expression
never varied. She was listened to with silent and respectful
sympathy. The dominant note of her speech was sorrow,
tempered with determination. She stood for the Republic.
She did not despair.

Interest quickened when Richard Mulcahy stood up
A rather slight and youthful figure, his voice, never loud
or assertive, is nevertheless penetrative, and he spoke in
a distinct and intellectual strain that made one listen to
him with intense interest. Nor was the speech less
absorbing in substance than in delivery. " What we
are looking for," he said, in that clear-cut, albeit gentle
voice of his, " is not argument, but an alternative." He
did not think de Valera's alternative had been given a
fair chance   On the other hand, he could see no other

road that Ireland could go except the path of this Treaty. They could have political chaos with or without war. He would prefer to see political chaos with war than the same thing without war.

Every word came slowly and earnestly, almost softly, from the thin lips, the sharp jaws, with the thoughtful eyes above, and the meditative brow shadowing the whole countenance. In my opinion, it was the ablest speech—from the point of view of pure intellect—delivered since the Dail assembled. There was no passion in it. There was no love or admiration for the Treaty in it. Neither was there the wild, whirling criticism of those who see nothing but degradation in the Treaty. The pith of the speech was this—is there a way out for Ireland except through the Treaty? He could not see it. That was the main point, and he pressed it home relentlessly, logically, and right up to the hilt. His reference to chaos on the Continent as the result of militarism, coming as they did from a man of war, brought minds back to a realisation of the terrible economic position of the world at present. France and Germany watching each other and ready to tear each other to pieces! Where was the gain to the world in that? Were Ireland and England to follow their example? Must they continue to kill the Compton-Smyths in self-defence? This touching allusion to brave men and brave enemies was understood by most present.

A low-sized, thick-set deputy with a pale face, but with strength of conviction written on every line of it, came forward to oppose the Treaty. It was Sean Moylan of North Cork. "I am a Republican," he said simply but firmly. This was the keynote of his speech. Every word of it was uncompromising. Richard Mulcahy had previously asked—What was the alternative? Sean Moylan from his point of view answered it. "Hands off the

Republic." It was uttered fiercely. But the peroration
staggered everyone who heard him. " If there is a war
of extermination waged upon us—I may not live to see
its finish—but by God no loyalist in my Brigade area
will see it either. It is time someone told Lloyd George
that." His voice throbbed with vibration caused by the
tremendous earnestness with which he uttered the words.
In thoughtful and grave humour the Deputies rose for
the midday interval.

When the House reassembled the avalanche of oratory
went on freshly as it did on Monday last. The first speaker,
Deputy P. J. Moloney, of Tipperary, set a commendable
example of brevity, but it was not followed. A vigorous
man beyond the prime of life, he said he was not going
to vote for the Treaty. " Damn the Treaty," he said,
" and what about the consequences."

Many of the speakers who followed seemingly forgot
that it is the month of shortest days in the year and that
life also is short.

Eoin MacNeill, intellectual, judicial-looking and deeply
read, descended from his Speaker's chair and made a
speech in favour of the Treaty. He declared that the ob-
jections to the Treaty now should have been made when
the Plenipotentiaries were sent over to London. With
hair brushed back over his thin features, he stood swaying
now and again, so as to face the House at all angles. He
spoke almost conversationally as if he scorned mere
rhetoric and only desired to make the actual position
perfectly clear. As he was analysing the various oaths
in his inimitable way I saw de Valera smile with broad
appreciation. It was good to see it because some of the
Deputies never smile. It is a pity.

The rest of the speaker's address was a learned but
clear appreciation of what the Treaty actually conferred

on Ireland—equality of status and sovereign power in her
own domain. Arthur Griffith manifestly listened to this
masterly exposition with keen interest, for he said, " Hear,
hear," more than once. It was certainly a statesmanlike
speech in the fullest degree—appealing, compelling, and
with a high constitutional tone in every sentence.

He denied that the Ministers of the Free State would
be the King's Ministers. The denial evoked applause.
He ridiculed the bogey of a Governor-General followed
about by flunkies and toadies. The real fact was that the
Irish Constitution would be based on the will of the Irish
people. It is only just to say that much of his speech from
this point was rather discursive and could easily have been
shortened.

Coming back to the vexed subject of the oaths an interlude occurred, Eamon de Valera again rising to explain
his position. There were cheers and counter-cheers. One
felt, however, we were entering the region of pure casuistry,
nebulous, unpalpable and unreal.

With all the zeal of a young and ardent barrister opening
his first great case Sean MacEntee rose to put the Treaty
in the dock. His head moved in sympathy with the
eloquent tones of his speech. The address was brilliant
but redolent of a type that I have heard hundreds of times.
It was a speech to arouse, to electrify, to move the feelings.
They were offered to surrender their aspirations—for a
price. He alluded in scornful terms to the price—he even
emphasised the word with burning contempt. In fiery
phrases he referred to Tone, to Mitchel, to Davis, and to
the men who had created the Republic in Ireland. He
folded his arms. He pointed dramatically. He placed
his hand to his side. History was full of great causes
wrecked by expediency. The resemblance to a great
college debating society was never absent as he spoke in

his melodramatic fashion. It was the speech of a young— a very young—man.

Every word almost was addressed to the emotions— to the shrines of the past, against compromise and expediency, and for principle, pure and simple. Towards the close of his speech he devoted himself to denouncing the partition clauses. A Deputy intervened, " Is the speaker prepared to coerce the Six Counties ? " This brought a quick but not a convincing answer from Mr. MacEntee, " I am not in the Government and I am not responsible for policy."

The orator proceeded with subtle modulation of voice and appropriate movements of head and body to develop his thesis. " This Treaty is the most diabolical onslaught." And sentence after sentence of flaming denunciation. Many of those present must have recalled '91 and 1901. " You who profess to be soldiers "—the words were directed to the army leaders who supported the Treaty. " Ulster will become England's fortress." The words were hurled forth, until the speaker almost became hoarse. " Double betrayal "—" violation of election pledges "— " I will not vote for this Treaty." With these words the speaker sat down.

After this torrent of passionate oratory, the mellifluous tones of Liam de Roiste in Irish were heard permeating the chamber with the soft breath of the South. When he spoke in English his voice became harder and sharper. " I took an oath to the Free State of Ireland, and I mean to keep it." He resented being told that he was making any spiritual surrender. If it came to the exact letter of the law, then everyone there was an opportunist. He underlined this point neatly. They were there by virtue of a British Act, and if they took their stand on principle, pure and simple, they would not be there at all. The real fact viewed by common sense was that Ireland was a sovereign nation—and recognised as such by the Treaty.

As the evening advanced several Deputies went into the lobbies to obtain a respite from the seemingly endless flood of rhetoric. The majority of the Cabinet and of the Dail, with heroic persistence, however, remained in their seats, and bore the ordeal with exemplary patience.

Liam de Roiste made an indirect allusion to this when he said the people in his constituency were for the Treaty, and were asking what was all the talk in the Dail about. The weary Deputies laughed and applauded.

Then with a timely allusion to the Christmas season at hand, he said that " peace on earth " was a nobler thing than any he had heard, especially when it could be had with honour.

For myself I think if he had concluded his speech with this beautiful sentiment it would, from an artistic point of view, have been more of a success. As it was, he went on to allude to Versailles and Washington and to world politics in general. Attention undoubtedly flagged.

Taken out of the tidal wave of words that enveloped them were some pointed phrases : " This is not a dictated peace. This is a negotiated peace." Dictated peaces had a habit of recoiling on the heads of the victors. Under the Treaty the Irish language would be made the soul of the Irish people. Under it also the plain people of the country could frame a Constitution in accordance with their wishes. The tricolour could be hoisted over Dublin Castle. From flags, the speech shifted to the theological aspect of oath. Finally, the speaker made an appeal for a Referendum so as to get the view of the Irish people on these proposals.

Then came the dramatic wind-up of the day's proceedings. The House was on the point of adjourning for tea when a crossfire opened between the opposing benches. From it emerged the definite fact that an agreement could not be reached even on such a minor issue as the length of the speeches and the division on the Treaty. Michael Collins expressed himself as ready for either alternative —either to adjourn over Christmas or sit night and day until they finished. He had sat up in London, and he could sit up in Dublin. This evoked from Madame Markievicz some remark about befogging and wrung from Michael Collins an angry and defiant negative.

Curiously enough she seconded his motion, and speaking with broken rapidity—the words coming forth in jerks— she said the lady members who had not the physique of the Minister of Finance, could not be expected to sit up night after night. A new complexion was put on the issue when Michael Collins said that for national reasons an interval was desirable. Interest therefore became acute as the first public division was taken. It resulted : For the Motion—77. Against—44.

Before the figures were announced a further indication of the rift was shown when the President raised a point as to the position of the Cabinet in the interval. A Deputy said the House would wish them to carry on, and this evoked applause and unanimity.

Eventually, to the intense relief probably of all present, the House stood adjourned to January 3rd, and to none was the relief more welcome than to the three score harassed Pressmen who had a fearful week dealing with the greatest Niagara of continuous eloquence in Irish history.

J. F. B.

CHAPTER VI.

AFTER THE RECESS.

Tuesday, January 3rd, 1922.

" How long, O Lord, how long ? " was the rather impious question we put ourselves after to-day's dreary debate

Before judging of our wickedness, consider the provocation. It is no light task for those who have not been present in the flesh to realise how wearisome is the whole performance. Even the members themselves now beguile the weary hours by reading their newspapers or having an occasional promenade along the corridor.

Repetition and irrelevancies are the besetting sins of Dail Eireann. Day after day members on either side rise to deliver themselves of arguments which we have already heard *ad nauseam* for or against the Treaty.

And the irony of it is that they all assure us that they are going to be quite brief. They did it the first day ; they did it until two days before Christmas, and they did it to-day. But if we except Brian O'Higgins and Sean McGarry, and perhaps one or two others, they all sinned again.

No doubt the members, realising their heavy responsibilities, are at pains to make their position clear in the eyes of their constituents. But we, poor sufferers, can only sigh and play with our fountain pens while the same old story is being told without even the merit of being told in a new way.

The plain, blunt truth is that there is scarcely a member who could not, with advantage to himself, to his own particular side, and to the public, have cut his speech by more than one-half. Just as a little exercise in mental gymnastics, it would be well if some charitable friend would winnow the chaff from the grain in some of the oratorical contributions.

Many of the members who have, so far, spoken have made several good points for the other side. And even to-day again we had the spectacle of bouquets being showered on the heads of some speakers—by themselves.

A fortnight has passed since Fionan Lynch protested against the indecent practice of " rattling the bones of the dead in the face of the Assembly." He was applauded from all sides of the house.

Four speakers out of five who have since spoken have also denounced the practice—and immediately proceeded to tell us whether Tone or Davis, or the Easter Week men, would have accepted or rejected this Treaty if the miracle of Lazarus were repeated.

The crowd which gathered before University College to-day was larger than on any previous day. But the atmosphere of uneasiness and anxiety had vanished. Even the Teachtai themselves, for some reason or other, looked more at their ease.

Michael Collins made a vigorous protest against un-punctuality at one of the sittings before Christmas, and at once there was a marked improvement. To-day things were as bad as ever. It was twenty minutes after the appointed hour before a start was made.

For some unaccountable reason there was no roll call before the debate, and no prayers were read, although Rev. Dr. Browne was in his place as usual.

Art O'Connor, Minister for Agriculture, delivered a

twenty minutes' onslaught on the Treaty. From his seat, behind de Valera, he smiled as if in challenge and in sarcasm across at Arthur Griffith and Michael Collins.

What, he asked, was the meaning of that promise by Arthur Griffith to the Southern Unionists ? and like the shot from a gun came the reply from Mr. Griffith, " Fair play."

He got rather mixed, I am afraid, in his metaphor when he spoke of " splitting a spectrum into fragments," and he gave Collins an opportunity of making a neat point against him when he spoke of " farmers' unions and people of that ilk who never did an honest day's work." Anyhow, he made it plain that his constituents need not attempt any dictation to him.

His best point was when he asked why the negotiations which had lasted for months could not have lasted a few hours longer to give the Plenipotentiaries an opportunity of consulting their Cabinet.

Piaras Beaslai provided us with one of the best reasoned pleas we have yet heard for the acceptance of the Treaty. To him the great point was the departure of the British army and the consequent freedom to build up the Gaelic State.

His speech bristled with posers for the opposition. " What you have called principles are really political formulas." " How is war to be avoided if the Treaty is rejected ? " And he neatly turned the argument against Miss MacSwiney when, in reply to her warning that demoralisation would follow the Governor-General, he asked if a shadowy representative without power or a soldier to back him would be more formidable than 50,000 British troops and 15,000 R.I.C. ? " People who fear such a calamity have no faith in the Irish nation."

Madame de Markievicz spoke for three-quarters of an

hour against the Treaty. Much of her speech could not be heard, as she turned away from the Speaker and the Press. She lacked her accustomed ease and composure, and was far from being as impressive as she is on a public platform.

She stood for a Workers' Republic as against this Treaty which was being backed by capitalists. Towards the end of her speech she made that poor joke which, by a strange irony, made Michael Collins stand out later in bold relief as the champion of woman against Madame.

The joke had not the merit of originality. The picture of Princess Mary as the bride of Michael Collins has been painted many times by would-be wits who have seen the strange turn events between Ireland and England have recently taken. Michael Collins was at his best when, after the adjournment, his loud, clear voice rang round the Chamber in protest against an insult which might cause pain to an English lady whom he did not know, and to an Irish lady who . . .

It would, however, scarcely be fair to think that Madame de Markievicz intended it as an insult.

J. J. Walsh nearly staggered us when he arose before one o'clock and calmly suggested that the Dail might consider the advisability of adjourning for lunch before his speech. " Two hours, at least," we whispered. But, no. He was quite moderate ; he was satisfied with a modest half-hour.

His strongest argument for accepting the Treaty was that the people willed it. " The public bodies which had asked for Ratification are as good Republicans as you are." And then we said a hearty " Amen " to his next point. " The Irish people are fed up with this ju-jitsu exposition of oaths." He might have added a lot of other things to the list.

However, he was not long in making it plain to us that his own particular method of handling oaths was the catch-as-catch-can style. He had, in fact, a very elastic mind on that matter. And those of us who remembered his defence of the Civil Servants whose oath of allegiance nearly split the G.A.A. in 1919, had to acknowledge his consistent elasticity in the matter.

He scored well off the Minister for Agriculture, when he defended the farmers as the backbone of the country in the fight. It does not require a very deep knowledge of the South and of its fighting forces and its ruined homesteads to realise how true that is to-day.

Brian O'Higgins set an example which other Teachtai might follow with advantage to everybody concerned. He was very brief ; he did not repeat the arguments of previous speakers ; he did not tell us what the resurrected dead would have done.

He was opposed to the Treaty because it was a surrender, and he denied the right of his constituents to act as the captains of his soul. But when he spoke of Robert Barton's admission that he, as a Plenipotentiary, had broken his oath in signing the Treaty, Arthur Griffith was fierce, fiery, almost angry. " Did we—did we break our oaths to the Republic ? " he roared, and with the licence and the gentleness of the poet, Brian replied by not replying, simply repeating that he had referred only to the case of Mr. Barton.

Ernest Blythe, the only member of the Dail, as he put it himself, who came of the people who are going to exclude themselves from the Free State, held that the Republic was not an end in itself, but was a means to an end. He would not be opposed to the coercion of Ulster, if it were necessary, and I think it was Michael Collins who said, " Hear, hear," to that.

One of the good points against the Treaty was made by Frank Fahy when he asked, in answer to those who declared the country was for the Treaty, would the men of 1916 have got a mandate from 10 per cent. of the people if they had asked it at that time.

George Nicolls, who proclaimed himself the last of the lawyers, didn't speak at all like a lawyer. He stood by the Treaty on the same grounds that, he said, the plain people of his constituency stood by it. His was the shortest address of the day, lasting only six minutes.

The Lord Mayor of Cork was disappointing. His contribution against the Treaty was weak. But when he spoke of compromise, he roused Collins to proclaim with biting sarcasm and emphasis that " the Minister of Finance had not compromised."

And then came the moment when we hoped that we were about to witness a dramatic turn which would yet save the Dail from division. It was when Michael Collins made the suggestion that the opponents of the Treaty should allow the Provisional Government come into existence and yet remain true to their Republicanism.

The features of every member of the Dail for the moment lit up with the light of hope. Even now, both sides would give much, very much to avoid the parting that is fraught with such danger and faced with such regret. But the opportunity was lost. Dare one hope that it will come again before they part ?

Seamus Dolan, brother to Charlie Dolan, who first raised the banner of Sinn Fein before the electors, fourteen years ago, is satisfied with the Pact. If the Treaty is rejected, he asked, where is your Constitution ?

Lorcan Robbins, in his blunt and straight-from-the-shoulder way of arguing, protested that the common people care not for formulas, but for freedom. Very properly, he emphasised the difficulty in which he and the others who supported the Treaty had been placed by the withholding of Document No. 2.

Sean McGarry promised us he would make a record in brevity. He didn't, but he went so near that we forgave him. Only ten minutes he took to tell us why he was voting for the Treaty. We howled with laughter when he said that if the members did not speak when Miss MacSwiney asked them at the private session some months ago they had made up for it since. They have, God knows, and the Irish people know.

P. DE B.

CHAPTER VII.

A DRAMATIC SCENE.

To-day's debate in the Dail began quietly, proceeded almost drowsily, but it ended in a heated scene that left everyone anxious and breathless.

The first speaker was a low-sized, whiskered Deputy from Kildare. Domhnall O Buachalla opposed the Treaty, and said the country was being stampeded, and what it needed was a tonic. I should have thought it needed a sedative, but there was this much to be said for the speech—it was brief.

Alec MacCabe, of Sligo, a tall, clean-shaven, clean-cut Deputy, read a very long speech in favour of Ratification. His allusions to Miss Mary MacSwiney and a reference to the extermination of the people for the sake of principle brought that lady Deputy to her feet with a protest. A further statement to the effect that the women of Ireland did not want a renewal of war also evoked dissent from another lady Deputy—he had no right to speak for the women of Ireland.

It was, however, the mention of Document No. 2 that produced one of those little interludes so frequent at sittings of the Dail. Mr. de Valera was on his feet in a moment, and passionately sought to make his position clear. He was ready to bring forward his proposal as an amendment.

"Are you ready to give it to the Press?" interposed Arthur Griffith. "I will move it to-morrow," said the President.

An appeal by Michael Collins for the non-interruption of the speakers and a plea for order in debate by William Cosgrave, brought a ruling by the Speaker that he would support Deputies who were speaking against interruption. Alas! The tendency to interjection again proved too much for members within even the next ten minutes.

Some novel points were made by Deputy MacCabe. He instanced Cuba, which was hedged around with restrictions of all kinds. "Not war, I fear," said the Deputy, "but ruin for Ireland if this Treaty is rejected."

The most pathetic speech delivered in the Dail was that of Mrs. Pearse. In soft tones, all the more poignant by reason of the emotion she felt, Mrs. Pearse spoke of her dead sons and declared they would have been against the Treaty.

Owen O'Duffy, of Monaghan, rose from his seat next to Michael Collins and in a business-like way explained why he favoured the Treaty. No party in the Dail, he said, had a sole monopoly of patriotism and this plain reminder evoked subdued approval. Another striking portion of his speech was an emphatic defence of the military members of the Dail—those officers who knew the strategic position and who had the courage to face the real facts.

Resembling in appearance his colleague, Sean MacEntee, there is a marked difference in the style of oratory of the two. Owen O'Duffy spoke without any attempt at eloquence, whatever, but his words, clear, lucid, distinct and sincere, reached every corner of the assembly. Especially was this the case in respect to Ulster. Here he was blunt and free from illusion of any kind. If there was a better policy to bring Ulster into an All-Ireland Parliament than that outlined in the Treaty—let that policy be brought forward.

Liam Mellowes followed. With fair hair brushed back, rugged countenance lit up by profound conviction and a rather discordant voice vibrating with the intensity of his beliefs he made a " no surrender " speech—totally against " this so-called Treaty." He believed in the Republic—and he pointed the finger of his right hand towards the Deputies to mark every word he uttered.

They were told they should respect the will of the Irish people. " Hear, hear," from Arthur Griffith. " All right," said Liam Mellowes, " I will read our Declaration of January, 1919, and I will make no apology for its length or for the time I take, either to the Dail or the Irish people."

" There," he declared, striking the table with his hand, " is the will of the people." His voice rose. " This Treaty abrogates the Republic." His tone was mordaunt. Now it became scornful. " The Republic does exist." De Valera with his finger to his chin was watching him intently as he spoke. " Let us face the facts," continued Liam Mellowes. " The people in the country are not in favour of the Treaty on its merits, but they fear what may follow its rejection."

There he said was the real truth. " It is not the will of the people. It is the fear of the people." He laid bitter emphasis on every word.

Despite the intensity of the speech, many Deputies were reading newspapers, and others interposed an occasional Hear, hear, with a burst of applause at intervals.

Desmond Fitzgerald, the Minister of Publicity, with his suave polished accent, was the first speaker after the luncheon interval. The Treaty brought them nearer the ultimate goal, and, therefore, he supported it in the interests of the Irish people. He scored a telling point when he said that Spain was a sovereign State, and yet had to submit to the occupation of Gibraltar by the British. His speech was a smooth, incisive and polished defence of the Treaty.

A young Deputy, James Fitzgerald, of Cork, in opposing the Treaty, declared that those who bore the brunt of the fighting were almost unanimous against the Treaty—war or no war. The people longed for peace, rather than for the Treaty. He spoke slowly, and rather hesitatingly, but somehow he made one listen to him with more attention than other orators whose opposition was couched in passionate vein. It was the first speech on the opposition side that sought clearly to answer the arguments of the Treaty on a practical, as apart from an emotional, basis.

" The compromise is not an ignoble one." So said Dr. Hayes, of Limerick, in supporting the Treaty. It was a necessary one. It was preceded by a whole series of compromises. The Republic ceased to exist four or five months before—but its ideal still existed, even in the hearts of those who supported the Treaty. Leaning forward, he said : " It is a bargain—and a good one." He quoted very effectively from John O'Leary. This Treaty was the beginning, the rebirth of Gaelic civilisation.

. A Deputy of powerful physique with a powerful voice, John O'Mahony, of Fermanagh, repudiated the assertion that the persons who were urging them to accept the Treaty were the people of Ireland. Letters or telegrams would not convince him. I gathered from his remarks that even if he found himself at variance with his constituents, he would vote against the Treaty first and resign after. At least that was how I took it that he interpreted his mandate. The burthen of his speech was that Deputies were free agents.

In a few delicious asides, Arthur Griffith said, " All right, John ! Who told me when I was going to London to bring back peace ? "

There were a couple of ripples of mirth and a little confusion, in the course of which the resonant voice of John O'Mahony was heard addressing the Speaker : " I consider you are not doing your duty." This brought the Speaker to his feet with the words, " Order, order." The incident ended in good-humoured laughter.

A breath of wholesome commonsense was wafted into the dreary afternoon's proceedings when Dan McCarthy, of South Dublin, blew the " rotten Press " and " packed Boards " story sky-high. The Press of 1922 was not the same as in 1916, and the old Boards of that time were wiped out. The public Boards were now Sinn Fein Boards —elected by the people, the same people who elected Dail Eireann.

Another thing he hammered home. " The 1918 election was not fought on the issue of an Irish Republic." With short, snappy phrase and scornful resentment he poured contempt on those people who were more Irish than the Irish themselves."

" I belong to the plain people," he declared defiantly. " and I don't care a d—— so long as we do good work for Ireland."

It was a dramatic speech. The people are for the Treaty, he said, and the best proof of that is—let them contest the country on it. " As for me, I am ready to fight the President for my seat, and I will bear him 100 to 1 on this issue. It is the same all over the country."

Dr. Ada English, with a refined accent, tackled the subject of the Oath in a refined way. One gathered it was a stumbling path for her, and the principal reason why she is against the Treaty. " A complete surrender," she said. With her hat off and her hand to her side she classed Lloyd George with the evil spirits, and in the next breath said, " We all want peace."

However, in a second we learned there were other things besides peace. Thus repetition and assertion followed one another, leaving one rather bewildered as much by her mode of delivery as by her mode of argument.

Deputy James Murphy, Drogheda, next explained why he was in favour of the Treaty. " I, for one, will not sacrifice the people to save my face." He chose the lesser of two evils.

The Drogheda Deputy's speech was brief. Dr. Cusack (Galway) set out to make a record in the same direction. Unfortunately his speech did not by any means create a record. It was a long denial of the fact that the Irish people had declared for the Treaty. There were voices for it, he declared, but not the constituencies themselves.

William Sears said to reject the Treaty would be political folly. " You talk of the Irish people as if they were fools," he said vehemently, " They are the shrewdest people in the world." Go down to the people and see. If this Treaty was before the people in 1918 or in 1921 what would be the result ?

" I say," he declared, " that the opponents of the Treaty have not 3 per cent. of the people of Ireland behind them." It was sheer madness to state the contrary.

From an ordinary defence of the Treaty the voice of William Sears rose until he delivered one of the finest speeches yet made in the Dail.

A couple of other speakers wound up the day's debate. It was during the speech of Deputy James Burke, of Tipperary, for the Treaty, that the really dramatic events of to-day occurred as in a flash. The Deputy was speaking of Document No. 2, when Mr. de Valera, with sparkling eyes arose and literally swept the chamber with the driving force of his personality. " I protested before, and I protest again," he declared. " about a misrepresentation of my position. I stand as a symbol for the Republic. Neither publicly nor privately have I lowered that position. It would be a matter for impeachment if I did."

One sensed the coming scene.

Said Mr. de Valera : " I didn't go to London because I wished to keep that symbol of the Republic pure even from insinuation, or even a word across the table that would give away the Republic."

" And I also protest," said Mr. Collins, springing to his feet, " that I have in any way given away anything."

And then when the adjournment was moved Mr. de Valera again intimated his intention of moving his amendment the next day. Arthur Griffith, pale but determined, faced him across the table in front of the Speaker. A document had just been put in their hands. It differed from another document of which they had heard something.

" You are quibbling," said Mr. de Valera, with flaming emphasis. Dan McCarthy interposed : " The President is a very touchy man, but there ought to be some decency in debate."

Arthur Griffith, persistent, kept on his feet and said that six clauses had been omitted from the document just now submitted.

Then Mr. de Valera spoke with every fibre of his long body tense and his head and shoulders bent forward. He uttered the words authoritatively. " I am responsible for the proposals, and the House will have to decide upon them. I am going to choose my own procedure."

Arthur Griffith spoke coldly, but intently : " The President has said he is going to choose his own procedure. This is either a constitutional body or it is not. If it is an autocracy let us know and we will leave it."

With these pregnant words he ceased speaking.

Thus the two leaders stood defiantly-looking, deeply moved and facing one another, in front of a thrilled Dail Eireann and a world array of journalists. A murmur of voices arises from the body of the Hall. The Speaker, who sat silently whilst the sharp interchange was in progress, now arose and said the only motion before him was that for the adjournment. Thus the scene ended for the day, leaving an anxious feeling over the commencement of the next day's proceedings.

And the representatives of the world's Press watched the scene silently and anticipated doubtless further developments that they could telegraph and cable to the ends of the earth.

J. F. B.

CHAPTER VIII.

A DAY OF SENSATIONS.

THURSDAY, JANUARY 5TH, 1922.

To-DAY was a day of dramatic events at Earlsfort Terrace. Not only on the stage but behind the scenes there were sensations and rumours of sensations.

At one time we had a section of the Press threatening to suppress the Dail, and at another we had the Dail threatening to suppress a section of the Press.

At the end, after a day of excitement and of rumour, we left with high hopes for the morrow. And we were not even wearied. For we had had more action than dialogue, and nobody even resurrected the dead or told us what would have been the attitude of Conor Mac Nessa towards the Treaty of Versailles or to the abolition of submarines, or whether Brian Boru would have allowed any restrictions on motor cycling.

When we entered there was nothing to indicate that we were to be spared another avalanche of oratory. But the air was thick with rumours and counter-rumours. A division was imminent—the Treaty was going to be rejected by two votes—the Treaty was going to be approved by four votes—no, there was going to be no division, one side was going to leave the House.

And in my hurry to get there in time I had not even glanced at my morning papers. At Earlsfort Terrace a copy of the leading article, so soon to be indicted, was thrust before my eyes.

" Did you read that ? "

No. But I read it then—and re-read it. And I wasn't by any means a prophet when my comment was : " Trouble ahead. They're asking for it—and they'll get it."

Meantime another document was sent round the Press benches for signature. 'Twas a protest against " the outrage perpetrated upon one of our colleagues " of the London *Times*.

He had been seized and carried off by armed men, and we were to ask Dail Eireann to have him released.

But our English colleagues who were so energetic in this matter could tell us no more. If his arrest had been unauthorised was it not sufficient to communicate with the Irish police ? And if his arrest had been ordered by the Irish Government, why should we interfere ?

These were questions that were not answered. And even though it was not exactly consistent, can we be blamed if we who had seen our own colleagues carried off by English forces, and our offices invaded by men wearing England's uniform at the dead of night to bully and threaten Irish journalists, pointed out that our English colleagues had made no protest against these things. Even in the wildest flights of fancy we could not imagine the reporters in the Gallery walking out of the British House of Commons because an Irish journalist had been taken to Dublin Castle. And so we, the mere Irish, did not sign.

After this little incident we looked at our watches to find it was half-an-hour after the appointed time, and the Speaker's chair was still vacant. But there was a good and sufficient excuse for the unpunctuality on this occasion,

Alderman Cosgrave was the first to rise in his seat to invoke the malediction of the House on the perpetrator of that stupid joke about ordering a Union Jack for Sinn Fein headquarters to celebrate the approval of the Treaty. The order for the flag came on the official notepaper of Sinn Fein. There was no such person as M. Whelan known to Padraig O'Keeffe, who ought to know every official at Harcourt St., and—but here the Speaker ended the matter, and the mystery remains unsolved.

Then came the bombshell. Sean T. O'Kelly broke the good news. A few of the members were having a little talk that might lead to agreement. Would everybody agree to give them a few hours more ? And everybody did with a fervent prayer that a way may yet be found out of a cruel dilemma.

And so, lightheartedly we were rising in our places when Desmond Fitzgerald raised a matter of urgency—but the Speaker was adamant. Had he known that the matter concerned the fate of the missing journalist he would probably have admitted the urgency of the case.

Michael Collins, Desmond Fitzgerald, Eoin MacNeill, and other prominent members of the Dail were at once beseiged by plenipotentiaries of the Press. And there were many explanations and assurances on both sides.

After which we proceeded to the Press room, where one of the foreign journalists solemnly proposed that the Dail should be boycotted pending the release of the missing man. And the Irish Pressmen had the effrontery to tell them some home truths and assure them that we had no intention of agreeing to any boycott since we had no reason to think that the Dail was in any way responsible And there for the moment it ended.

At half-past two came the first news from the missing

Pressman. He had arrived in Cork under escort, and his release would probably come within a few hours.

We were in our places again at three o'clock, but more than half-an-hour passed before the Speaker intimated that we might get our pens into action. This time again 'twas Alderman Cosgrave, but he was on a different topic now.

Speaking with evident feeling, he drew attention to the personal attack which had been made on de Valera and Erskine Childers in the leading article of the *Freeman's Journal*.

The writer had actually assured Ireland that its trusted leader " has not the instinct of the Irishman in his blood," while Mr. Childers was, in plain words, only an ex-spy.

Never before have I seen indignation painted so clearly on the face of every member of Dail Eireann. Even some persons in that portion of the House reserved for strangers were so carried away as to applaud Gavan Duffy's references to " this infamous attack."

Member after member on both sides of the House rose to add his voice to the condemnation, and to speak his faith in and love for de Valera. Sean Etchingham went so far in his resentment that he gave us a synopsis of the history of the *Freeman's Journal*, and proposed that its representatives be expelled from the House.

But, while one could sympathise with his feelings, it was difficult to see how that step could be justified, since the representatives of that paper present were no more responsible for the leading article than they were for the advertisements.

The better judgment of the House prevailed. The Press should get every liberty, but it should not have a licence to insult any member.

" We stand for the liberty of the Press," said Desmond Fitzgerald, and every member applauded.

" The Press has a right to say what it likes," said Arthur Griffith, with emphasis. And so the matter ended, very properly, with a dignified protest.

Sean Milroy provided us with a little interlude. There were, he alleged, personal attacks in another paper also, which he held in his hand, but he could not, he said, very well suggest that the representatives of that paper be excluded.

We craned our necks to see what the paper was. It looked suspiciously like the *Republic of Ireland*, and we wondered how the House would receive a motion to expel Liam Mellowes, journalist, without interfering with the privileges of Liam Mellowes, Deputy for Galway.

During the debate on the subject Harry Boland entered. He had landed in Ireland but a few hours before. With the same boyish smile as he wore when he used to step from the pavilion to the playing pitch at Croke Park with his caman in his hand, he looked as fresh and hale as ever, and as he passed to his seat he was greeted with loud cheers, even from those who believe he is going to vote against them.

" Personal explanations " are now becoming a regular feature of the Dail's proceedings. We had several again to-day.

John O'Mahony had to deny Arthur Griffith's allegation that John wanted " peace anyhow." But Arthur only said, " All right, John," and the members roared.

And John sat down and probably he and Arthur will be as close and as staunch a pair of comrades as they have always been. It is thus that our members agree to differ, and it is this happy atmosphere of brotherhood that makes the possibility of permanent division all the more poignant.

De Valera, too, made a personal explanation. When he spoke of using " his own procedure " on Wednesday evening he had unwittingly used a phrase open to misconstruction. He had no intention of imposing his will upon the House. " None can say I am an autocrat."

A few minutes later we had a wordy battle between the opposing chiefs. De Valera and Griffith had a few words to say about " breaches of confidence " and " quibbles," and for a time we had fears ; but, as on so many previous occasions, the old camaraderie prevailed.

The next sensation was Frank Drohan's resignation. His views differed from those of his constituents in Tipperary. He, therefore, saw no honourable course open but resignation.

Commandant O'Duffy gave us a message of hope before the adjournment. Substantial agreement was reached on a number of vital questions discussed by the unofficial peace committee.

Can this committee which at the eleventh hour has attempted to bridge the chasm complete its task ? With one voice Ireland will pray that it may.

P. DE B.

CHAPTER IX.

DE VALERA'S RESIGNATION.

JANUARY 6TH, 1922.

NEVER before in its chequered history has Dail Eireann provided scenes of excitement, outbursts of passion and stormy protests such as we witnessed to-day.

When we entered the Council Chamber at three o'clock there was little outward sign of the storm that was brewing. But once more the air was thick with rumours of yet more sensations to come.

At 3.20 p.m. the Speaker took the chair. De Valera, looking more haggard than I have ever seen him before, was sitting at his table with his heavy overcoat closely buttoned. He seemed—as indeed the event proved—to be assuring himself that some weighty decision he had taken would for ever stand the test of conscience.

When the Speaker entered de Valera at once rose and approached the chair. For several minutes he was engaged in earnest conversation with Prof. MacNeill. Then the drama began.

'Twas 3.30 p.m. when de Valera opened his address. At most times he speaks with a rapidity unusual in a statesman. To-day he spoke with that slowness and deliberation which are the mark of a man who has weighed well the meaning of the consequences.

Not a sound broke the stillness save the clear, one might almost say musical, voice of the Irish Chief. Every ear was strained to catch every sentence, every syllable. We had reached a crisis in the long drawn-out debate.

" This body has become completely, irrevocably split." That was the preface to the half hour's review of the history of Ireland since 1916.

If he was to defend the Republic he must get a free hand and be no longer hampered by the division in his Cabinet. That was the reason of his proferred resignation.

And then in tones almost pathetic he brought us back to the days when he entered politics as a soldier. As he detailed the growth of the Republic he raised his hand from time to time and fiercely, even violently, emphasised his points.

If ever there was one for a moment to doubt the sincerity, the transparent honesty of the Irish leader, that doubt would pass with one glance at the man as he stood before his colleagues.

His resignation, which he was now placing in the hands of Dail Eireann, involved the resignation of every member of the Cabinet. There we could not follow him. For there is an anomaly in his position.

De Valera, as the ordinary pedestrian understands his position, is not only President of the Republic, but Prime Minister. Now, though he is a man who rarely leaves any doubt in one's mind as to what he means, I must confess I did not understand what he meant by resigning his position as Chief Executive Officer.

Did he mean his position as President or his position as Prime Minister, or both ? The anomaly arises from the fact that in no other country is the President also Prime Minister.

According to usage in other countries the resignation of the Prime Minister involves the resignation of his Cabinet. The resignation of the President involves no such consequences. We need go back little more than a year to the time when M. Deschanels resigned the Presidency of the French Republic, but the Cabinet remained intact.

However, that is by the way.

No doubt it was that " infamous attack " on himself and his colleague, Erskine Childers, that de Valera had in mind when he passionately refuted the suggestion that he was not Irish of the Irish. " I was reared in a labourer's cottage here in Ireland," and never did we feel so proud of the personality of the man who has led us to the threshold of freedom as when he made that passionate outburst and revealed his soul as he had never previously done.

And as he read that passage from the Constitution of Sinn Fein, denying the right of any foreign power to claim allegiance from the Irish people he dashed the document on the table and fiercely declared that he at least would never become a British subject.

De Valera sat down. In a moment half-a-dozen deputies were on their feet. Arthur Griffith, Dan McCarthy, Michael Collins, and several others, angrily protested against the interference with the procedure. The resignation of de Valera was drawing a red herring across the track.

Dail Eireann might arrange its own House in its own way, but this was a question of life or death for the Irish nation, and, as Dan McCarthy said, " The nation is bigger than any man."

Michael Collins sprang to his feet. With blazing eyes he drove home the great blow against de Valera.

" I offered my resignation and he refused."

Where was the urgency now, if de Valera did not consider the division in his Cabinet of urgency when the session opened ? " We will have no Tammany Hall methods here," and the pro-Treaty party applauded uproariously.

Standing erect before the Treasury table, the Finance Minister was now defiant, scornful, challenging.

" The House was prevented from receiving the report of a committee by three bullies."

Then the Speaker, with unexpected firmness, intervened. The term " bully " must be withdrawn.

Michael Collins paused. He sought inspiration in the documents before him. Again there was tense silence. Anxiety was written on every countenance. Would Michael refuse to withdraw ? Would there be a scene ? Was there material for a fatal rupture if the Minister of Finance remained obstinate ?

Almost a minute passed. And still not a word.

Then slowly, deliberately, and with emphasis, Michael Collins spoke :

" I can withdraw the term—but the spoken word cannot be recalled "—and with school-boyish naivety Michael looked at the Speaker, and added, " Is that right, sir ? "

If you were yourself one of the members to whom that term could apply, what could you say, what could you do ?—Obviously, only one thing. And they all did that. They rocked with laughter. Your Dail member, like every other Irishman, can enjoy a witticism.

Cathal Brugha followed. His retort to Michael Collins was bitter, almost venemous.

Padraig O'Maille and Harry Boland had made several vain attempts to get the ear of the House. Now they were speaking simultaneously. We could catch only a word here and there from either of them. Then Padraig gave it up. " Lean leat," ar seisean le Hannrai, agus do shuidh se sios.

And when Harry had spoken, Padraig was again on his feet to demand why this position was not brought before the House at the beginning of the session. " This procedure is treating the Irish nation unfairly."

Peadar Hughes, of Dundalk, contributed. And his contribution received the unanimous approval of the House, the Press, and the Strangers.

" I am Chairman of a Board of Guardians," he began. And the House laughed to its heart's content. But when Peadar had finished the laugh was on his side.

" And if the Board conducted its business as this House does, I would be ashamed of it."

Never since the session began was truer thing said. And just as we do not often read the reports of boards of guardians, we began to wonder what type of individual is he—if any, indeed, there be—who at this stage sits down, of malice aforethought, to read the full report of the Dail meetings in his morning paper.

A minute later de Valera said the next truest thing. " I am sick and tired of politics—sick to the heart. I have only seen politics within the last three weeks."

He is not half as sick of these politics as the Irish people are. They, too, have seen politics enough in the last three weeks—enough to satisfy this generation, and probably to annoy the next.

A few minutes later the fragments of the great bomb-shell had been removed. There was to be no suspension of the order of the day and no resignation. The discussion of the Treaty was to be continued, and, by common consent, to be expeditiously concluded. May God fortify the members in the latter part of that resolution.

So the talking was resumed. Dr. Ferran began by asserting there was no such thing as a Treaty ; but, strange to say, he took half-an-hour to attack it,

The Mayor of Waterford believed there was a Treaty, and he was satisfied with it. Ten minutes was all he required to tell us why.

Next came Commandant Robinson, from Tipperary, to denounce the Pact. The army was opposed to the Treaty, he said, and de Valera protested against introducing the views of the army, but Seumas very neatly retorted by pointing out that they were not ordinary soldiers, for if they had not political views they would not be soldiers at all.

He was followed by another officer, Commandant-General Gearoid O'Sullivan, who defended the Treaty. If one were not actually looking at the face of the speaker, one might be forgiven for thinking the voice was that of Michael Collins. And when Gearoid taunted the Irish speakers with being incapable of conducting this debate in Irish, the Speaker challenged this view. It could be done in three months if they started now. To which Gearoid very cleverly replied that the start will be made when the Treaty is ratified.

Deputy Derrig, who also opposed Ratification, quoted Harold Cox against the financial clauses   I wonder he did not see the absurdity of relying on such an authority on matters of Irish finance. But he scored when he pointed out that if the national movements in Egypt and India owed anything to Ireland it was to the example of the Irish Republic and not to that of the Free State.

" My conscience, my constituents, my country." These were the arguments of Ald. Staines in favour of Ratification. And he, like Deputy Aylward, who followed him on the other side, was pleasantly brief. How we could wish to see the others follow their example.

The Mayor of Wexford, another supporter of the Treaty, has also learned how to turn the tables on an opponent. " Don't we send the Connaught Rangers and the Leinsters to oppress the Indians to-day ? " he asked, " and how can the Republican Government prevent it." And he, too, was brief and to the point. And there ended the eighth day of the public debate.

P. DE B.

CHAPTER X.

THE FATEFUL DIVISION.

SATURDAY, JANUARY 7TH, 1922.

THE curtain has rung down. The first act in the drama of a nation's life has ended. But the picture of that last awe-inspiring scene, with its mingled pathos and exultation, with its fears and hopes crowding thick upon us, will not soon fade from the hearts of those of us who witnessed.

For weal or woe the spokesmen of the Irish people have made their choice. The weary, sleepy, drowsy debate is no more, and the future—— ? Bright, we pray, but not without its perils.

We who had sat and listened from the beginning even unto the end during these days, big with the fate of Ireland, took our leave with a sigh and a prayer. For in that gloomy, crowded chamber it was given to us to see those things which few may witness but which will be writ large in the annals of our time.

The features of each member as he took his place this morning bore outward sign that we were nearing the climax. They told plainly of the responsibility so soon to be faced. Even those who had yet to give us their views did so with a suggestion of apology for delaying the momentous decision.

Harry Boland opened with a well-reasoned attack on the Treaty. He was followed by Joe McGrath with an equally effective defence. Ten other speakers who followed claimed between them only an hour, while one of them was actually content with two minutes.

When we re-assembled at 4.15 Daniel Corkery, in a blunt denunciation of the Treaty, created a record by resuming his seat after less than two minutes. Three Donegal men followed, only one of whom made us impatient.

Then came two of Cork's soldier members—Tom Hunter and Sean Hales—taking opposite sides, but wasting very little time to tell us why.

At five minutes past five Cathal Brugha rose to make the final onslaught on the Treaty.

Do labaiṗ ré aṗ dtúiṗ aṗ ƷaeḋilƷ aƷuṗ aouḃaiṗc ré náṗḃ ṁian leiṗ feaṗƷ do cuṗ aṗ éinne aċ Ʒo Ʒcaicṗeaḋ ré an fiṗinne do ṗáḋ aƷuṗ do ṗéiṗ an cṗean-ḟocal, aṗ ṗeiṗean, bíonn an fiṗinne ṗeaṗḃ.

He spoke much about Michael Collins and the Army, but while many of the pro-Treaty members interrupted now and again Collins remained unmoved. "Anything that can be said about me, say it," was his only remark.

Dan McCarthy was of opinion that the Minister for Defence should not be interrupted, as he was making a good speech—for the Treaty, which drew the rejoinder, " Ʒcoḃaimíd an deiṁniú aṗ ṗin aṗ ball."

At 6.20 Cathal Brugha concluded, having spoken for just an hour and a quarter. His speech was that of an uncompromising Republican, but he passionately resented the statement that he wanted war.

At 6.25 the House adjourned. Arthur Griffith was quite willing to conclude the debate, but de Valera, with characteristic gallantry, urged that it would not be fair to Griffith to continue without an interval.

Meantime a vast crowd had assembled before the building, and the number who had gained admission was larger than ever. When we returned at seven o'clock several of the Pressmen found their seats had been seized by strangers, and protests were unavailing, because these strangers were the friends of somebody or other, they were told.

It was a strange crowd that was present at that last sitting. Members of the Standing Committee of Sinn Fein, with the Lord Mayor of Dublin, occupied the front seats. Behind was a battalion of journalists, drawn from every corner of the globe.

In the body of the Hall were Volunteers and civilians, men and women, old and young. A sprinkling of clergymen, too, and an ex-member of the Irish Party, while " Æ " appeared for the first time to take his place beside a coloured student. That veteran sponsor of Sinn Fein, ex-Ald. Cole, was seated beside a Divisional-Commandant of the Army.

A few heated though friendly interchanges between Harry Boland and Michael Collins, and Arthur Griffith arose. He spoke for just an hour and five minutes.

Never before have I heard Arthur Griffith deliver such a powerful speech. Never for a moment did he become personal, never for a moment lose his coolness or depart from the solid rock of argument.

Every argument put up against the Treaty, every argument in favour of the alternative, he tore to shreds to the satisfaction of his supporters, and hurled back into the faces of his opponents.

His tributes to Michael Collins were uproariously applauded. " He was the man who fought the ' Black and Tan Terror,' and the cheers were deafening.

Is this a final settlement, he was asked, and his reply was crushing—" It has no more finality than we are the final generation on the face of the earth "—and again his supporters roared their applause.

Mr. Griffith declared that the number of adjectives used in denouncing this Treaty was unparalleled since the days of Biddy Moriarty. Some of the British Pressmen appeared to think that the deceased was a member of Dail Eireann, or had at least taken an active part in recent Irish politics.

Whispered inquiries were made across the desks as to how her name should be spelled and what, we were asked, had she done in the war. On learning that Biddy's sole claim to fame was her skill in handling a particular variety of English, our American and English confreres hastily expunged her name from their records.

Once only the opposition were roused to fierce resentment. They dare not face their constituents, he challenged them to oppose this Treaty.

Sean T. O'Kelly sprang to his feet. In a moment Erskine Childers, Maire nic Suibhne, Madame de Markievicz and half-a-dozen others had risen in their place to accept the challenge.

At 8.30 he had finished. Five minutes later the Speaker rose to take the fateful vote.

Diarmuid O'Hegarty, standing on the left of the Chair, held the roll in his hand. The assembly was hushed, awestruck, almost ceasing to breathe. Even outside the crowd seemed to have realised that the hour had come, and the voices became stilled.

The roll-call began. County Armagh was taken first. " Micheal O Coileain— ? "

Michael Collins rose from his seat. Slowly facing the Speaker, he spoke.

" ır coıl " (for).

And so Diarmuid went through the list of one hundred

and twenty members, each rising in his place and responding, "1ᴛ ᴄᴏɪʟ" or "ɴɪ ᴄᴏɪʟ."

The name of the County Down Deputy was near the top.

"Eamon de Valera— ? "

"ɴɪ ᴄᴏɪʟ" (against).

And the voice was that of a man who is an unwilling witness to a great tragedy, a man who stands over the coffin of one whom he loved above all else in this world.

The Deputies for Cork were being called out. Again came the name Micheal O Coileain.

There was a pause. Diarmuid looked across for the reply. There was none.

Another pause. Then Michael Collins rose again.

"The Deputies on the other side need not wait. I—have—already—given—my—vote." And so he was claiming no second vote for his second constituency.

A moment later the name of Eamon de Valera was called out for Clare. He shook his head slowly and deliberately, and smiled across at Collins. He, too, had given his vote.

Within a minute, Arthur Griffith was facing the Speaker. His name had been called for Tyrone-Fermanagh. He demanded the Speaker's ruling.

"One man one vote."

And again Griffith was on his feet to protest against the disenfranchisement of his second constituency, and Sean Milroy, in his deep, thunderous voice, joined in the protest.

Meantime strangers, Pressmen and officials were slowly ticking down "For" or "Against." Our foreign colleagues, who knew not the tongue of the roll-call, could only appeal to us for the signal.

How painfully slow was that ceremony! Once only did we lose our seriousness. It was when Sean Etchingham responded with a " Ní toil " with such an emphasis on the " Ní " as might have hurled the Treaty across the Irish Sea to Downing Street.

One man we waited for. It was Dr. McCartan. He would refuse to vote, he told us a fortnight ago, because the Republic was dead. When his name was called, he stood up, and bending forward towards the Speaker, uttered the words, " Is toil."

Only two were missing—Tom Kelly and Larry Ginnell. The name of Frank Drohan, who had resigned, was not called.

The Speaker's name was called for Derry. With his eyes fixed on the paper before him he never moved, uttered not a sound. Diarmuid looked at him for a reply.

Taking in his hand the printed copy of the Standing Orders the Speaker read.

" The Speaker shall vote only in case of a tie, when he shall have a casting vote."

And the roll-call proceeded.

The last name had been called—Prof. Stockley. And at 8.45 Diarmuid Hegarty sat down.

There was another pause. Pencils and pens were working feverishly to make the totals. Two minutes passed.

Suddenly a mighty cheer was heard outside. The waiting crowd had got the result even before the Speaker had had the totals placed in his hand.

And so it was. The motion for the approval of the Treaty had been carried. The Speaker made the announcement.

De Valera, whose features now wore a deadly pallor, addressed the House in a broken voice :

" The Republic still goes on until the nation has dis-established it."

Michael Collins next, with a moving appeal for unity and a noble, generous declaration of love and faith in his chief, de Valera.

But the division was now irrevocable. Maire Nic Suibhne, almost sobbing but still defiant, denounced the " betrayal."

De Valera was again on his feet.

" I should like to say my last words. . . . The world is looking on at us now——"

And he stopped. The minute's silence was painful. The sentence was unfinished. De Valera fell back into his seat.

The strong man who had defied the might of an Empire, faced its armies, and scorned its jailors—had broken down.

It was an awful moment. Women were weeping openly. Men were trying to restrain their tears. Some because of the approval for the Treaty—but all because of the final parting in that body which had won the love of Ireland and the respect of the world.

We rose to depart. A young man amongst the " strangers " shouted for three cheers for the " President of the Irish Republic," and men and women on all sides responded.

We waited vainly, hoping that before they parted that a Joint Committee would be formed. But it was not so, and we wondered if even now it is not possible to repair the link that has snapped and weld it once more to give it that strength which once made England's steel shiver to pieces before it ?

As we walked down the stairs from the Council Chamber the crowd was gathering close in the hall. Some were cheering, some were boohing.

A Volunteer officer appeared on the scene, and there was silence.

"You are here by the grace of the University authorities," he said, turning to the visitors. "And you shall neither cheer nor booh."

And that is the spirit we need to-day more than ever.

P. DE B.

CHAPTER XI.

DE VALERA'S DEFEAT FOR PRESIDENCY.

JANUARY 9TH, 1922.

UP to last Saturday evening it was like a see-saw. One speaker for the Treaty and one against. To-day it was like a jig-saw puzzle. But it is a puzzle to which a clever player can already discern the clue that will bring the pieces together again.

At the opening Eamon de Valera, who presented clear traces of the great emotional strain through which he has passed, rose to tender his resignation as President. His face was pale and he spoke in low, ordinary, collected tones. He was heard in sympathetic silence.

Then Michael Collins stood up to make his suggestion once more for a Joint Committee for Public Safety. " Let us stop talking," he said emphatically, " and get on with the work. The real problem we are faced with now is that of taking Ireland over from the English."

Eamon de Valera intervened :

" This Sovereign Assembly must have an Executive."

Sean MacEntee, whose resemblance to a barrister one can never forget, declared that the opponents of the Treaty could not become willing agents in the subversion of the Republic. This put an end to the suggestion of Michael Collins for joint action.

What was to follow ?

The slight figure in deep black of Mrs. Clarke uprose,

and in a faint voice she proposed the re-election of Mr. de Valera. In more strident tones Liam Mellowes seconded. The issue was now knit.

The attitude of the pro-Treaty Deputies was revealed when Padraic O Maille, in indignant accents, asserted that this procedure was treating the Irish nation very unfairly. Why was not notice given ?

" We are not children," said Michael Collins, intervening. " We anticipated something of the kind. My suggestion is designed to meet it." He jerked his head back defiantly. " I talk straight," he added with powerful emphasis.

" People will regard us as a laughing stock unless we do something. Do it. On with the work. That is my way."

Phrases that will become historic in Ireland !

He swung his powerful arms as if to suggest that he was tired of all this talk, and wanted action instead.

Miss MacSwiney also brought reality into the debate, when in clear-cut language she said :

" We believe in the existence of the Republic. That Republic is not dead. Until the people of Ireland have disestablished that Republic it continues in being."

This put the issue plain early in the day.

Mr. Gavan Duffy asked Mr. de Valera about his policy in case he was re-elected. Swinging his tall, sinewy body forward de Valera explained his position. Dail Eireann as the Sovereign Parliament of the nation needed an Executive having the confidence of the House. It was their duty to maintain the independence of Ireland during the interval before the will of the people could again be manifested.

And then came the vital words—the words everyone was expecting.

His Government, declared Mr. de Valera solemnly,

would not, if he were elected, interfere with the work of those who were taking the further steps necessary to give effect to the Treaty. " Let them go ahead." In the end, the people having the full facts, would be in a better position to decide.

For a brief space the Assembly strove to get the full bearing of this momentous utterance.

Then Deputy Hogan, from a back seat, speaking with intense feeling, denounced the proposal. " Let us be honest," he said, passionately. " If you re-elect a President to fight this Treaty speak no more of Constitutionalism— Dictatorship—tyranny—call it anything save constitutional government."

De Valera's face worked with obvious resentment during this speech. " I am not offering myself," he said, indignantly, " but, as I said before, you must have an Executive."

Deputy Sears said they had the Hertzog precedent in South Africa for the out-and-out Republicans. Why not stick to the constitutional way of governing Ireland when the governing lay in their own hands and not any longer in that of England ?

A different line was suggested by Sean MacEntee. Why not re-elect Mr. de Valera as a protection against English treachery. A similar course was outlined by Sean T. O'Kelly. Why disestablish the Republic until at least every ounce that could be got out of the Treaty was obtained ?

All these suggestions evoked scornful comment from Deputy Cosgrave. The minority of an assembly to carry on the government by consent of the majority ! Was the like ever heard ?

De Valera grew restless under it all. " I am only putting myself at your disposal. Go and elect your President."

But Mr. Cosgrave was not to be moved. " We are told to go ahead with our work. If you adopt this course you are taking every care that we cannot go ahead with that work."

The puzzle was very perplexing at this moment.

It was not rendered easier by a little aside with Sean MacEntee. How it arose does not matter, but clearly it must have originated in the reported resignation of the young Monaghan Deputy. But Sean MacEntee tartly interposed : " I never said I would resign." Roars of laughter.

Deputy Cosgrave : " If you speak until you are understood it will take a long time." Renewed laughter.

Further references by Deputy Cosgrave to Mr. de Valera not realising the situation under which the minority would dictate policy to the majority brought de Valera to his feet with blazing eyes and the three words flung at his political opponents : " A deliberate misrepresentation."

Deputy Cosgrave held to his points with merciless logic. Did they desire an autocracy ? Were they afraid of the people ? There were eager cries of " No, no." " Well, I am glad of that," said Deputy Cosgrave, good humouredly.

He ridiculed the assertion that it was the fear of the people, not the voice of the people, they were getting. It was the good sense of the people. He wanted things done in a constitutional way—without bitterness.

Richard Mulcahy, in quiet tones, said they had carried on before without a President. The main thing was to get their hands on the resources of Ireland—to take them over from English control. " That," said Mr. Mulcahy, impressively, " is what we are determined to do."

Always direct in utterance, Sean Milroy spoke of the

" sheer exasperation " of reversing on a Monday what they did on a Saturday. The personality of de Valera was being used to defeat the will of Dail Eireann and the people of Ireland.

Mirth greeted an apparent slip of the Deputy when he said a Minister's duty, if defeated, was to resign. " That was what the President was doing "—so interjected a member. Clearly, however, what Deputy Milroy meant was resignation—not re-election afterwards. " It will be no laughing matter if this Treaty is defeated." There would be no smiles in Ireland then.

Madame Markievicz said she stood for the Republic and re-election of the President.

Liam de Roiste, Dr. Cusack and other deputies followed, and Prof. Stockley spoke of misunderstandings. At this point they were clearly pardonable. No one knew exactly where they stood.

Clearly many things were possible. " One effect of all this," said Liam de Roiste, " is that British forces may still remain in the country." Deputies heard this in silence.

Speaking in impassioned tones, Sean Etchingham denied that they would abrogate the Republic. In God's name he appealed to them to keep the Republican Government alive and watchful.

" The sooner we have a plebiscite or a General Election the better," said Kevin O'Higgins earnestly.

But his colleague, Ernest Blythe, did not think an appeal to the people would be on a full issue at present. A Constitution would have to be framed first. What mattered just now that they were heading straight for a situation of the most dangerous type. Were they to have two distinct governments ?

The speech of this hard-headed Northerner was the last heard before the mid-day adjournment.

In the afternoon, Austin Stack, in a blunt speech said the Republic still existed, and he supported de Valera—the biggest man in Europe and one who would never let them down. In the end the free choice of the people would have to be obtained—the Republic or this document of Mr. Griffith.

" Bad tactics, from the point of view of the nation "—this was the view of Michael Collins. " There is going to be an end of it—fairly and squarely," he continued with tremendous energy. " There should be no tactics in an hour like this. You are putting the President in an impossible position. Let us be honest."

Cathal Brugha, in quiet accents, made a brief allusion to his speech on Saturday evening. The war was not won by any one man. There was a little breeze between himself and Michael Collins over signed or unsigned cheques, but it passed.

The main things, said the Minister of Defence, was that they had a mandate and would carry it out. " We don't want to interfere with you or your Treaty," he said, pointing at the other side, " but you also do not interfere with us." No hindrance, but no co-operation—this was Cathal Brugha's speech in a nutshell.

Seumas Fitzgerald, of Cork, said a large portion of the Army was against the Treaty. Let the majority party proceed—but let them not interfere with the Dail.

Speech after speech followed, one Deputy comparing the situation to a Free State with a Punch and Judy show in the rere. They would not have that.

" I would not like to see a dog shot for the difference between the Treaty and Document No. 2."

And so on. " Leave our Republican Government intact until it is disestablished by the Irish people," said Sean MacSwiney, of Cork.

" If we have two Governments," said Deputy Dolan, despairingly, " a clash will come."

Piaras Beaslai, turning to the Assembly, with anger darting from his eyes, said : " What this means is that you wish to wreck the Treaty, and you know that well. The men who advise it are no friends of de Valera.

Then Arthur Griffith, who sat silent all the morning and afternoon, rose to press home what Deputy Beaslai had stated. " The people using de Valera know what they are doing." " This would lead to chaos of the worst type. Two sets of Governments ! " It would lead to absolute chaos.

De Valera intervened. The Republic would constitute the reserve for the nation. Certain departments were vital to it if Ireland were to be safeguarded.

Sean McKeon said the will of Dail Eireann had been expressed. It was for that he had stood in the dock. If that will is now flouted, " then I was the damnedest fool that ever stood in a dock."

Then came the dramatic division : 58 for de Valera ; 60 against. The result was heard by a hushed house. Eamon de Valera was no longer President of an Irish Republic !

A remarkable scene followed. Griffith was on his feet with a generous tribute. " This is not a vote against de Valera."

Speaking with smiling friendliness, with relief I fancied, de Valera accepted the thunders of applause that greeted his rising with graceful, almost boyish delight.

The talk of fratricidal strife was, of course, all nonsense. He had said before, " You will want us yet." He said it again.

Even to get this thing the men and women with him would yet be needed. " And I tell you we will be there with you against any outside enemy at any price," he said amidst a wildly enthusiastic House.

Had the Assembly adjourned after this great, noble-hearted, warm-hearted utterance it would have parted for the day in splendid spirits.

As it was, it hung on for another dreary hour or so and in the end postponed the sequel.

J. F. B.

CHAPTER XII.

GRIFFITH ELECTED PRESIDENT.

Tuesday, January 10th, 1922.

A useless and irrelevant debate—dramatic exit of the minority party—election of a new Cabinet—a more harmonious afternoon sitting, and a wholesome clearing of the air.

Having completed this programme, Dail Eireann, to the satisfaction of the members and of the public, has ceased talking.

It began in the usual leisurely, humdrum fashion. The appointed hour was 11 o'clock, but we generally stroll in now about half-an-hour later. There is never the slightest danger that anything will happen before that time. Punctuality has never been our national virtue.

First we had the Pope's message of joy "because of the understanding or agreement." And addressed to the President of Dail Eireann, too.

Evidently, we remarked, de Valera's little reminder to the Vatican a few months ago has had its effect. The Cardinal Secretary of State is learning to be more careful in his phrases and more mindful of Irish susceptibilities.

A few minutes later and Michael Collins was proposing Arthur Griffith as President of Dail Eireann. De Valera having resigned, the ship wanted a captain. There had already been too much talking, and they wanted to get ahead. That was his plea.

Incidentally he told us about what he called the " Black and Tan " methods employed against the *Cork Examiner*. It is only a few days, we recalled, since both sides of the House vied with one another in proclaiming their burning desire to defend the freedom of the Press.

Commandant O'Duffy, second sponsor for Arthur Griffith, said, " Get on with the work." We vainly hoped his example in saying just what he wanted to say, and no more, would be followed. Alas, we have now resigned ourselves to our fate.

Nearly two hours' discussion followed. Almost everything but the motion was talked about. Occasionally, in our righteous indignation, we looked towards the Chair to see if there was a Speaker. There was.

Sean MacEntee did not think a signatory to the Treaty should be President. Then he gave us a historical analogy from the days when John Redmond tried to capture the Volunteer movement.

" When Mr. Asquith was going to trick an Irish Constitutional Nationalist the people sprang to arms in his defence." I am afraid it is a poor compliment to the Irish Volunteers of 1914 to suggest they were going to risk a drop of their blood for the contemptible Home Rule Bill. The pledge of the Volunteers at that time was to defend the " rights and liberties common to all the people of Ireland," and not to defend John Redmond or his " charter of liberty."

Then followed a series of questions from de Valera and others of the opposition to Griffith asking how he could reconcile his appointment as President of Dail Eireann with his intention of carrying out the terms of the Treaty.

There was no ambiguity about Griffith's reply. He would keep the Republic in being until the Free State was established. It would be his duty to carry into effect

the will of the Sovereign Assembly regarding the Treaty ;
then the people could choose between the Republic and
the Free State. But apparently the opposition were not
satisfied.

Miss MacSwiney would have Griffith give an undertaking that he would not merge the office of President
with that of head of the Provisional Government. Even
de Valera broke into a hearty laugh at the impossible plan.

Possibly some of the deputies expect Mr. Griffith to
affix to the doorposts of his official residence two brass
plates on one of which he will be described as—

PRESIDENT OF DAIL EIREANN.
OFFICE HOURS, 10 to 12.

And on the other—

HEAD OF THE PROVISIONAL GOVERNMENT.
OFFICE HOURS, 2 to 4.

Questions were being hurled at Griffith from every
corner. Liam Cosgrave mildly drew attention to the
usual procedure in Parliaments, but still the thing
continued.

The discussion gradually drifted into a repetition of
the old story about the signing of the Treaty until Arthur
Griffith was roused to fierce resentment by a remark of
Sean Etchingham's, which Griffith, with biting emphasis,
and with an angry flash at the Wexford Deputy,
characterised as " a damnable lie."

Even the members themselves were now wearied by
the debate.

" Vote ! Vote ! Vote ! " cried half-a-dozen members
simultaneously.

De Valera was on his feet and facing the Speaker. He spoke slowly and deliberately.

" As a protest against the election as President of the Irish Republic of the chairman of the Delegation, who is bound by the Treaty conditions to set up a State subversive of the Republic, I, for one, will leave the room."

In an instant all his supporters had jumped to their feet. De Valera turned to the right and walked slowly from the room.

Everywhere there was confusion and excitement. The supporters of the Treaty remained seated, but the minority hurriedly marched for the door.

" Deserters !" " Traitors !" " Cowards !" " Foreigners " Such were the epithets hurled in scorn and defiance from minority to majority, and from majority to minority, while journalists and strangers looked on in silence at the amazing scene.

Every member who had voted against the Treaty left the Chamber. Commandant Barton joined them. Dr. English turned from the door to smile sarcastically at the occupants of the now sparsely filled benches. David Ceannt stood for a moment before departing to wave a paper in his hand and shout " Long live the Republic ! "

Sean Etchingham was the last to go. As he was leaving Michael Collins crossed the floor to intercept him for some purpose or other, and for a brief moment they confronted one another. Then Michael Collins returned to his table.

The whole scene lasted two minutes. Then all was quiet again. None of the strangers went to the corridor to follow the movements of the minority. Once more all eyes were on the members who had remained.

Several Deputies hurriedly crossed the floor to whisper to one or other of the Plenipotentiaries. Another minute and the House resumed its business.

The Speaker, as calm and unperturbed as if nothing had occurred, put the motion. Arthur Griffith was unanimously elected President of Dail Eireann.

Then, with business-like rapidity, he nominated his Cabinet. Only two, Michael Collins and Liam Cosgrave, retained their offices. And with fears and misgivings, we adjourned for two hours.

Again we made no haste to be in our places at 4 o'clock, and again we were right. It was nearly half-an-hour later when business was resumed.

De Valera and his followers were in attendance. There were some who had assured us they would never return, but they did not know the spirit that guides Dail Eireann— minority no less than majority.

Tom Johnson introduced a Labour deputation to call attention to the question of unemployment and other no less pressing economic problems. He spoke briefly and very much to the point, and his reference to Labour's share in the national struggle were generously applauded.

And the Labour deputation had left within a quarter-of-an-hour with an assurance from Arthur Griffith that definite steps would be taken.

The worry and strain of the past few weeks have left their mark on de Valera even more heavily than on the other Deputies. His brow is more clouded and his features more pallid. His voice, too, has lost much of its ring, and he speaks with less of his old fiery energy.

He could not, he said, congratulate the new President. And as he went on we saw more clearly what his future relations shall be to the majority party in the Dail.

De Valera's followers will not stand in the way of Arthur Griffith, but they cannot recognise the other Government of which he will be head. They will continue their own policy, but Griffith can count on their support in dealing with any foreign Power.

Arthur Griffith's future policy was again outlined to the House. In the main it was an amplification of his statements earlier in the day.

Dail Eireann is going to remain in existence until the Free State has an election. " All I ask is that we shall not be obstructed." " If the people turn down the Free State for a Republic, I shall back them."

Like Eamon de Valera, he is tired of politics. " I would like to get back into private life." He and his colleagues have a mighty task to face. " Only give us a chance."

Erskine Childers and Piaras Beaslai simultaneously sought the eye of the Speaker. The one wanted to put a question, and the other wanted to know what was before the House.

Dan McCarthy, mindful of a previous experience, would like the Speaker to rule a discussion out of order—if it was out of order—before they had wasted a few hours on it.

But Erskine Childers was not to be denied. He put a question to Arthur Griffith.

For the first time Griffith lost his temper, and we were sorry.

" I will not reply to any d—— Englishman." And he banged the table with his clenched fist and glared across at Childers, whose retort that Griffith might with more effect have banged the table before Lloyd George, drew roars of applause from the anti-Treaty party, and drew from Griffith the rejoinder : " I banged the table before your countryman, Lloyd George."

The incident ended at that. Arthur Griffith has since the negotiations began gone through a trying ordeal.

That is, perhaps, the excuse that may be offered for the incident, for wherever Erskine Childers may have first seen the light, Arthur Griffith will probably be the first to admit that he has done a man's share in the work for Ireland.

The next item to be discussed was de Valera's motion to declare that the Treaty could not be the basis for an enduring peace, and to make counter-proposals to Britain. The whole question of the Treaty would have been re-opened if the Speaker allowed the motion.

De Valera's good sense saved an awkward situation. He withdrew his motion.

The Speaker's motion, reaffirming that Ireland is a sovereign nation, was all that remained to be debated. There was nothing in it conflicting with independent Republicanism, and Eoin MacNeill expected no opposition.

De Valera thought otherwise, and another awkward possibility was avoided by the withdrawal of the motion.

Before we parted, Griffith made another touching appeal for a fair chance. " For three months," he said, " we have been working night and day." And when he referred to de Valera he spoke of President de Valera, adding in a tone which betokened his regret that it was not so, " I still call him President de Valera."

At a quarter to six, after eleven days of public session, Dail Eireann adjourned. The members seemed no less pleased at the respite than the public and the weary Pressmen. And withal we carried with us the impression that the last few hours' debate has cleared the air of many misunderstandings and given renewed assurance that both parties, going their own way, will, as of old, do their best for Ireland, working not only towards the same objective, but where possible marching along the same road.   P. DE B.

CHAPTER XIII.

ARD-CHOMHAIRLE.

JANUARY 12TH, 1922.

AFTER the storm comes the calm. After Dail Eireann comes Ard-Chomhairle. The delegates assembled this morning in the Oak Room of the Mansion House, Dublin. Perhaps the fiercely cold weather had something to do with the atmosphere of peace and fellow-feeling that prevailed. Certainly there was not a jar in the proceedings. Pro-Treaty advocates and anti-Treaty advocates sat and talked and voted without the smallest indication of bitterness or animosity or acute party feeling.

Even the coming split was discussed without a trace of partisanship. Ard-Chomhairle has set a headline to the nation in the critical days that lie ahead.

Ard-Chomhairle represents over 1,200 Sinn Fein clubs all over Ireland, and some that are outside Ireland. It meets not later than seven weeks after the annual Ard-Fheis, and its principal duty is to complete the Standing Committee, in which the Executive power of the Sinn Fein organisation is centralised.

Eamon de Valera is President of this organisation, and he was early in his place this morning. He swung into the chair lightly, almost buoyantly, flinging his heavy brown overcoat from him. But, faith, he soon put it on again. The cold was too much even for him.

There was no sharp separation of comrades because

of political differences. Austin Stack worked side by side in friendly co-operation with Padraic O'Keeffe though they are both T.D.'s and voted apart in the Dail. Arthur Griffith, founder and inspirer of Sinn Fein, came in so quietly, and sat all day so quietly, that he scarcely made himself observed. He bore even on his solid, square-built, strong face manifest signs of the tremendous days through which he has lived, and of the awful responsibility cast on his shoulders. He only spoke once or twice, and then very briefly.

Eamon Duggan sat beside him, but did not speak at all. Neither did Michael Collins, who came in about noon, looking tired, worried and pre-occupied. Mrs. Pearse was present, but listened and did not speak. Harry Boland alone seemed blooming. The morning session was spent in discussing credentials, and in making arrangements for the election of the Standing Committee. The only sign of the rift was the appointment of five tellers on each side—that of Eamon de Valera and Arthur Griffith. This was done quietly, very friendly, to tell the exact truth.

It was during the afternoon, when the delegates re-assembled, this time to shiver in the cold immensity of the Round Room, that Mr. de Valera sprang the grand surprise of the day. And even that surprise did not arouse the assembly to anything more than mild interest. Briefly, Mr. de Valera said they had got to face facts in that organisation, as elsewhere—and the one overmastering fact was that they were split asunder on fundamentals. They had kept together up to now—a sort of Coalition— but now that Coalition was burst in twain. That was the position in front of Sinn Fein.

I must say he stated the case with splendid clearness, lucidity and broadminded tolerance. He was more than fair to the other side—as a matter of fact he somewhat understated his own side in order not to permit the smallest trace of ill-feeling or personal rancour towards his opponents. But he made it plain that with a division inevitable it was better to face it like men rather than try and work together in an impossible combination.

I do not wonder at the devotion of his followers to de Valera. His personality is a lovable one. It was never more apparent than yesterday. Would to God the country could come through its differences in the future with the same lofty charity that marked Ard-Chomhairle to-day !

There was a general discussion on Mr. de Valera's proposal. Some thought it was too sudden. Others that Ard-Chomhairle could not decide off-hand on the matter. Eventually a shrewd, kindly-eyed priest from the West of Ireland, Canon Moran, of South Galway, I think, solved the difficulty by suggesting that an extraordinary Ard-Fheis be summoned to decide on the future of the organisation. This was agreed to by all sides. Suggestions followed as to the best means of summoning this assembly, consisting of nearly 3,000 delegates.

About five o'clock Arthur Griffith emerged from the obscurity of a back seat, went on the platform and held a whispered conversation with Eamon de Valera. Evidently it related to nothing more important than the urgent calling away of Mr. Griffith, for Mr. de Valera made that plain a little later. The announcement of the election of the Standing Committee was made to a thin House. Mr. Griffith's followers secured a great majority. But there was no bitterness on the other side. The result was taken in sporting fashion.

This practically concluded the business of Ard-Chomhairle, but the proceedings did not terminate without two manifestations, one somewhat humorous and the other very serious. The former consisted of more than one sly hint that the country is sick of words—of talk, of speeches. Get to work. De Valera evoked cheerful laughter by paraphrasing Collins. The other related to the position of Nationalists in the Six Counties. One Ulster delegate bluntly suggested that they had been let down by both Free Staters and Republicans. I gather that Sinn Feiners in the Six Counties will not see the rest of Ireland divided without taking action to see that they themselves, at least, are united against their lifelong enemies.

J. F. B.

CHAPTER XIV.

TREATY FORMALLY RATIFIED.

It was a simple, brief, and businesslike affair, this laying of the foundation-stone of a new edifice of Government.

Like the members who met to approve the Treaty of Peace, Dublin, too, was cold and formal. The Mansion House has acquired a magnetism which the idle and the curious of our Capital can never resist. But to-day the crowd which stood to watch was small, unusually small; only a few hundred spectators in all, silent, unemotional, almost listless.

The camera men alone showed signs of excitement; to them comes no peace, no truce. Heedless of the on-coming cars, they lay in ambush in Dawson Street to take deadly aim at the half-dozen young girls who marched in silent protest to and fro with their anti-Treaty placards held aloft.

Not at all becoming the dignity of a nation's legislature is the Oak Room. Dark, gloomy, forbidding, it can comfortably accommodate four score men. And so the latecomers with their notebooks had to huddle and cramp where they might.

Yet there were things for which we were grateful—punctuality and brevity. Within five minutes of the appointed hour a start was made; fifty minutes later still and the Oak Room was deserted.

The Ministers of Dail Eireann occupied the seats close to the Chair. The rank and file of the Dail majority party were in the body of the hall. In the front row were the four Trinity College members, two sitting on either side of Padraig O'Maille.

It would have broken the heart of Lord Carson to see these chosen ones of his old constituency chatting most affably with that fighting man from Connemara. And they didn't seem a bit afraid of him, nor even look suspiciously to see if he had a gun in his pocket, and I never once saw Padraig make the Sign of the Cross. We Irish can get on remarkably well if friend John would only cease interfering in our family affairs.

What pleased me most of all was the amount of Irish spoken. There were those who would have us believe that Piaras Beaslai and Liam de Roiste and Padraig O'Maille would forget their Gaelic when they came in contact with the Trinity College atmosphere.

There was more Irish spoken in that fifty minutes to-day than I heard during a week of the Dail sittings. Even the Trinity men caught the spirit.

It started with the roll-call. Every name was in Irish, and every member present answered " Annso " until we reached the names for Trinity. Then, as if to show our bi-lingual tolerance, we returned to the harsh Saxon sounds again. But our new members were not to be outdone in this spirit of give-and-take, and a broad, happy smile broke over the countenance of every man there when Professor Alton and Mr. Fitzgibbon unhesitatingly flung out the response " Annso."

Only a mere trifle, perhaps. But who dares not hope that it is symbolic of the rapprochement, the better understanding to come ?

There were no speeches. That is to say, anything

that was said had to be said, and nobody attempted more.

Liam de Roiste, in the rich Gaelic of the South, explained the object of the meeting, and Piaras Beaslai, without unnecessary preliminaries, moved the approval of the Treaty.

A few minutes more, and the Provisional Government was appointed. Of the eight, we noted, six are Ministers of Dail Eireann, but neither the President nor Minister for Defence was included.

Arthur Griffith, in a two-minutes' address, held out the hand of friendship to every Irishman, and Professor Thrift, on his part, no less willingly responded.

A few minutes more and the historic assembly approved the minutes of its proceedings, and the chairman had signed what was in effect both its birth certificate and its death certificate. And thus, after nearly three hundred years the record established by the Short Parliament of Charles I. was broken for ever.

Before the members filed out to face the camera I saw the four Trinity men in friendly conversation with Arthur Griffith and the Minister for Defence. Such a scene needs no comment.

P   DE   B

THE DIVISION,

The following is the historic division list :—

FOR THE TREATY—64.   AGAINST—57

MUNSTER.

CORK CITY.

ALD. J. J. WALSH   MISS MARY MCSWINEY
ALD. L. DE ROISTE   D. O'CEALLACHAIN

CORK MID., N., S., S.E., AND W.

MICHAEL COLLINS   SEAN MACSWINEY
SEAN HAYES   DANIEL CORKERY
P. O'KEEFFE   SEAN NOLAN
SEAN HALES   SEAN MOYLAN

CORK EAST AND NORTH-EAST.

                                THOMAS HUNTER
                                DAVID KENT
                                JAMES FITZGERALD, JUN

CLARE COUNTY.

SEAN LEDDY   EAMON DE VALERA
PATRICK BRENNAN   BRIAN O'HIGGINS

KERRY AND LIMERICK WEST.

PIARAS BEASLAI   AUSTIN STACK
FINIAN LYNCH   CON. COLLINS
J. CROWLEY   E. ROCHE
                               P. S O'CAHILL
                               T. O'DONOGHUE

LIMERICK EAST AND CITY

DR. HAYES   MRS. O'CALLAGHAN
WM. HAYES   M. P. COLIVET

TIPPERARY MID., NORTH AND SOUTH.

SEUMUS BURKE   ALD. JOS. MACDONAGH
                               P. J. MOLONEY
                               P. J. COUNT O'BYRNE

WATERFORD COUNTY, CITY AND TIPPERARY E.

DR. VINCENT WHITE   CATHAL BRUGHA
                               SEUMUS ROBINSON
                               EAMON DEE

LEINSTER.

CARLOW AND KILKENNY.

ALD. W. T. COSGRAVE
GEAROID O'SULLIVAN

JAMES LENNON
E. AYLWARD

DUBLIN COUNTY.

FRANK LAWLESS
G. GAVAN DUFFY
DESMOND FITZGERALD
P. DERHAM
J. O'DWYER

MRS. PEARSE

DUBLIN CITY.

JOSEPH MCGRATH
PHILIP B. COSGRAVE
RICHARD J. MULCAHY
MICHAEL STAINES
DANIEL MCCARTHY
ALD. SEAN MCGARRY

ALD. CHARLES MURPHY
MADAME MARKIEVICZ
PHILIP SHANAHAN
ALD. MRS. T. CLARKE
ALD. SEAN T. O'KELLY

KILDARE AND WICKLOW

ROBERT G. BARTON
C. M. BYRNE

ART O'CONNOR
DONAL BUCKLEY
ERSKINE CHILDERS

LEIX AND OFFALY.

DR. PATRICK MCCARTAN
KEVIN O'HIGGINS
JOSEPH LYNCH
EAMON BULFIN

LONGFORD AND WESTMEATH

JOSEPH MCGUINNESS
SEAN MCKEON
LORCAN ROBBINS

LOUTH AND MEATH.

E. J. DUGGAN
PEADAR HUGHES
ALD. JAS. MURPHY
JUSTIN MCKENNA

J. J. O'KELLY (" SCEILG ")

WEXFORD.

ALD. R. CORISH

DR. JAMES RYAN
SEAN ETCHINGHAM
SEUMUS DOYLE

CONACHT.

GALWAY COUNTY.

PADRAIC O'MAILLE
PROF. J. B. WHELEHAN
G. NICOLLS, SOLR.
P. J. HOGAN, SOLR.

DR. BRIAN CUSACK
LIAM MELLOWES
FRANK FAHY

LEITRIM AND ROSCOMMON N.

J. N. DOLAN
ANDREW LAVIN
T. CARTER

COUNT PLUNKETT

MAYO S., AND ROSCOMMON S.

WM. SEARS
D. O'ROURKE

HARRY BOLAND
THOMAS MAGUIRE

MAYO, NORTH AND WEST.

JOSEPH MACBRIDE

DR. CROWLEY
P. J. RUTTLEDGE, SOLR.
THOMAS DERRIGG

SLIGO AND MAYO EAST.

ALEX. MCCABE
THOMAS O'DONNELL

FRANK CARTY
DR. FERRAN
JAMES DEVINS

ULSTER.

ARMAGH COUNTY.

CAVAN COUNTY.

ARTHUR GRIFFITH
PAUL GALLIGAN
SEAN MILROY

DOWN COUNTY.

DERRY CITY.

FERMANAGH-TYRONE.

SEAN O'MAHONY

MONAGHAN COUNTY.

ERNEST BLYTHE
EOIN O'DUFFY

SEAN MACENTEE

TIRCONNAILL.

JOSEPH SWEENEY
PETER J. WARD
DR. J. P. MCGINLEY
P. J. MCGOLDRICK

SAMUEL O'FLAHERTY

NATIONAL UNIVERSITY.

PROF. MICHAEL HAYES

PROF. W. F. STOCKLEY
DR. ADA ENGLISH